Three Minutes a Day

VOLUME 46

THREE MINUTES A DAY
VOLUME 46

Tony Rossi
Editor-in-Chief

Gerald M. Costello
Contributing Editor

The Christophers
5 Hanover Square, 11th Floor
New York, NY 10004

www.christophers.org

Jesus said, "Not everyone who says to Me, 'Lord, Lord,' will enter the kingdom of heaven, but only the one who does the will of My Father in heaven...Everyone then who hears these words of Mine and acts on them will be like a wise man who built his house on rock. The rain fell, the floods came, and the winds blew and beat on that house, but it did not fall, because it had been founded on rock."

MATTHEW 7:21,24-25

The Christophers warmly thank
all our friends, sponsors and supporters
who have made this 46th volume of
Three Minutes a Day possible.

We offer our special appreciation
to the following for their
contributions to this book:

Margaux Stack-Babich

Joan Bromfield

Abigail Caperton

Monica Ann Yehle Glick

Sarah E. Holinski

Karen Hazel Radenbaugh

Stephanie Raha

Julie Robison

Matthew Wormer

Dear Christopher Friend,

It's a joy for us to bring you the 46th volume of the *Three Minutes a Day* series! Our intention is to share with you the hope and light that are at the heart of the Christopher message.

Like all Christopher activities, this series is able to be a part of so many people's lives thanks to dear friends like you. You are our family and, because of you, we are able to share stories of encouragement, faith and love in a world that can seem very dark at times.

The other day, one of our Christopher friends called our office just to ask us to keep her intentions in our prayers. Our staff went right into motion, circling together and praying for her. We are honored to be a part of your lives. Thank you for being a part of ours.

May God bless you and your loved ones always!

Mary Ellen Robinson, Vice President
Father Dennis W. Cleary, M.M.

What Goes Around Comes Around

What would you do if you found a laptop and a backpack containing an envelope with $3,300 in cash in a train station?

For homeless Arizona man Dave Tally, the prospect of getting his hands on this much money was tempting, but in the end, his conscience prevailed. "It wasn't easy, but I know [returning] it was the right thing to do," Tally told *ABC News.*

The flash drive in the laptop determined the backpack belonged to Bryan Belanger, an Arizona State University student who had intended to use the money to purchase a used car from Craigslist. Nothing could describe Belanger's immense relief when he recovered his property within five days. "It's just the greatest thing I've ever experienced," he said.

Because of Tally's good deed, Belanger not only gave him a cash reward but also offered to volunteer at the Tempe Community Action Agency where Tally holds a part-time job.

Always make an honest effort to do the right thing.

So whoever knows the right thing and fails to do it, for him it is sin. (James 4:17)

Lord, grant us the strength to do the right thing.

Finding Purpose in Suffering

U.S. Army Sgt. J.D. Williams' life changed the day he stepped on an improvised explosive device (IED) in the Kandahar Province of southern Afghanistan. According to Sgt. Williams, the blast launched him 20 feet in the air and left a six-foot crater in the ground. At a hospital in Germany, the young soldier found out that he would need to have his right arm and both legs amputated.

After his surgeries, Sgt. Williams was sent to an Army medical center in Texas to recover. There, his parents, along with his wife and one-year-old daughter, watched as he received the Purple Heart from his hospital bed.

Throughout his recovery, Sgt. Williams has been thankful that he stepped on the IED himself instead of one of his fellow soldiers. He believes he is a lucky man and has said, "I really think God has a purpose for me on this planet. I will find it, whatever it is."

During times of suffering, know that God is with you.

I consider that the sufferings of this present time are not worth comparing with the glory that is to be revealed to us. (Romans 8:18)

Give me the strength I need each day, Lord, to be courageous and delight in Your plan for me.

Doing What You Can

A mother of two wanted to help others while also being able to stay home with her youngsters. So she started small—and went on from there.

Lisa Klein of Rockridge, California, decided to donate baby clothes to new mothers in need. She started with her own children's clothing, but the project grew as word spread and she made new connections. The former advertising professional spoke to women's groups, created an online presence and developed a network of volunteers.

Willing staff members at hospitals and birthing centers now distribute donations. They identify low-income families and others temporarily down on their luck. One new mom lived in a bus. Another woman came from Algeria and had no family in the area.

Families are grateful for the clothing and the support. Klein's children are also involved. When her youngest outgrows something she says, "Let's put it in the baby box."

Is there a project you and your family might do together?

Stretch out your hand to the poor, so that your blessing may be complete. (Sirach 7:32)

Spirit of Love, grant me the grace to serve Your people cheerfully every day of my life.

Clean Water, a Precious Commodity

When clean water is readily available, it's easy to underestimate the importance of a regular uncontaminated supply.

Dave Huebsch, founder of Rising Villages and Common Hope in Guatemala, says that installing water lines costs less than the medicines needed to treat the illnesses caused by dirty water.

"It's also cheaper than buying caskets," a local resident pointed out.

In parts of the world where water is rationed, people are at risk for skin and gastrointestinal problems. The ravages of war cause many problems. In some cases, it is diarrhea which kills.

A priest who served in the Democratic Republic of the Congo said that villagers fleeing from military conflict lose access to water. They may escape into the bush for long periods of time, eating poorly and drinking contaminated water.

Fix that leaky faucet. Contribute to aid organizations. Appreciate how precious abundant clean water really is.

Those who drink of the water that I will give them will never be thirsty. (John 4:13)

We take so much for granted, Holy Redeemer. Encourage us to be alert to the problems of neighbors everywhere.

Outsmart Yourself

You've probably heard of the placebo effect: the brain's power to create a sense of physical wellness with the help of an external aid that, in reality, provides no benefit.

What's less studied is the other side of the coin, what writer Leslie Goldman calls the "*nocebo* effect...or thinking you're ill when you're perfectly fine." The brain anticipates a negative outcome through the power of suggestion: for example, a hyperawareness of normal aches and pains. Goldman offers us tips for avoiding this problem.

- Focus on a positive outcome.
- Assess your symptoms rationally. Instead of chalking up a stomachache to some health scare in the news, ask yourself if you felt ill already.
- Talk with your doctor or pharmacist, who can help you assess and understand your true risk of side effects.

Use common sense concerning your health and other essential matters that affect you and your family.

May the Lord of peace Himself give you peace. (2 Thessalonians 3:16)

Blessed Trinity, help us to see ourselves and our bodies as they truly are, and to embrace a positive attitude.

Don't Fit In? Don't Worry!

During a recent interview on The Christophers' radio show/podcast *Christopher Closeup,* singer and songwriter Audrey Assad recalled that she felt like a misfit when she was in middle school.

A hard-working student who enjoyed being in the school band, Assad never quite fit in. But in retrospect, she believes that was a good thing.

"At the time, I hated it," said the singer who was 2010's top-selling new Christian artist. "Now I look back and think it's been a valuable lesson. It showed that God had a plan for me all along. You don't have to fit into any kind of peer group to be used in the kingdom, to do valuable things, to do life-changing things. God uses us with all our quirks and with all our faults as well."

Consider how God wants to use you today. Then do your best to live out His will.

You are precious in my sight and honored and I love you. (Isaiah 43:4)

Remind me not to seek the approval of others, Holy Savior, but always and only Yours.

State of the Art

The annual festival held by VSA—the International Organization on Arts and Disability—displays the artwork of children with disabilities such as autism, dyslexia, and cerebral palsy in a popular exhibit titled State of the Art. Now, the 51 winning entries are going on tour across the nation.

By showcasing the talents of these children, the group challenges people to find inspiration in the passion and skill of those we far too often see merely as objects of pity.

Consider Amanda LaMunyon, whose acrylic painting of the scissortail, Oklahoma's state bird, earned a place in the exhibit. Before she began painting, many children didn't want to be around her because of the effects of her Asperger syndrome. But after they recognized her talent, says her mother, "They saw her through different eyes, and they were more accepting of her."

Don't let disabilities blind you to the true nature of a person. Treat each person you meet as someone with something special to offer.

Be kind to one another, tender-hearted. (Ephesians 4:32)

Lord of All, help me to see each person I meet as a uniquely gifted part of Your creation.

Trying to "Peace" Together Hope

During one recent year, the once beautiful and serene city of Jos in Nigeria was wracked with violence. Repeated religious conflicts left many dead, property destroyed, and lives shattered.

Seven people died, and four were seriously injured in one such attack. A man who lost his wife and children told the Catholic archbishop there that he had forgiven the harm done him; the head of the village declared the same.

"We keep encouraging Christians not to lose faith in God nor be paralyzed by fear and anger, but rather to renew their love for God and neighbor," explained Archbishop Kaigama. "Each of us is called upon to be an agent of peace and reconciliation—and then hope will surely come."

Are you angry with someone, or even with yourself? Take a moment today to work toward forgiveness.

In everything, do to others as you would have them do to you; for this is the law and the prophets. (Matthew 7:12)

Help me, Lord, to make more room in my heart for love.

Improving Life Expectancy

When Brian Mattson learned that his life expectancy was just 52, he was understandably upset. He had used an internet tool called Vitality Compass which calculates life expectancy based on diet, exercise and other key factors.

Mattson was already 38 years old, and admitted his poor habits: "Most nights I'd come home and watch TV and eat junk food."

That was in 2009. Since then, Mattson has shared his discovery with other residents of his community, Albert Lea, Minnesota.

Today, as a community, Albert Lea residents work together to get healthier. Moraa Knoll is now 30 pounds lighter and has made new friends. John and Jackie Abrego traded junk foods for fruits and vegetables, and have not only improved their health but have saved money.

No one is an island. Connecting with others can improve your health and state of mind however long you live.

Take care of your health. (Sirach 18:19)

Teach us to weave bonds of love and care in our communities, Loving Father.

Parents of 500 Children

Russ and Rita Hoffman began their mission to care for homeless and orphaned children by seeking to adopt a single sibling for their biological daughter. But when the agency suggested that the couple adopt a young set of triplets, the Hoffmans quickly agreed. "I think God put a desire for babies and young children in my heart," says Rita.

This love of children inspired the couple to later adopt two more children, and ultimately become foster parents to more than 500 others. Over the course of 45 years, the couple has opened their door to children of all races, ages, and abilities.

While the prospect of such a commitment might appear daunting to some, Russ says, "The love just comes naturally. There's nothing to be afraid of."

Real love is selfless, fulfilling the soul in countless ways. Love without reservation.

Receive the kingdom of God as a little child. (Mark 10:15)

Inspire us, Spirit of Love, to love unconditionally.

Kiss and Tell

People from everyday folks to performers to presidents were asked their secrets for healthy longevity in marriage in a *Wall Street Journal* article. Their strategies are worth noting.

- Find the middle ground. Strong couples credit compromise as the definitive strategy for overcoming problems.
- Be funny. Many couples rely on humor to neutralize potential conflict and remind one another of their love.
- Keep (some) secrets. Deep trust allows for some personal space as long as it does not threaten or isolate the other person.
- Never, ever give up. Don't throw in the towel at the first sign of trouble. Recognize what's worth fighting for in the relationship and work at it.
- Stay Alive! Do your best to stay healthy and to help your spouse stay well, too.

A happy marriage takes attention and work from both partners. But the results are more than worth the effort.

I am my beloved's and my beloved is mine. (Song of Solomon 6:3)

Eternal God, in a time of uncertainty, help us to recognize what we can accomplish together with hard work and love.

A Hundred Years of Service

James H. Carrigan has lived 100 years and has a few things to teach about prayer, faith, friendship and service.

"I wake up and I say my prayers," said Carrigan, an usher in his New Jersey church. "I usually go to 12 o'clock Mass every day. I keep going because I am coming up to the end of my term, you know? I want to be prepared."

Faith has always played an important role in his life including the years he spent serving in the Army in Europe during World War II, and while Carrigan and his late wife raised three children. Even after retiring he remained active in church, the senior citizen center and the Knights of Columbus.

Asked about his longevity, Carrigan says, "Three square meals a day, seven hours of sleep each night and good friends."

Stay active and involved in life for however long God gives you on this earth.

I will praise the Lord as long as I live; I will sing praises to my God all my life long. (Psalm 146:2)

Grant me the desire and ability to live with zest and joy, Spirit of Love.

Dreaming Big

Challes Reese dreams of gracefully moving across the stage as she performs beautiful dance routines.

In reality, the 15-year-old has cerebral palsy, a neurological condition that impairs muscle control, and uses a wheelchair to get around. But that doesn't mean she can't dance. Reese entered dance team tryouts at her Dubuque, Iowa, high school in her motorized wheelchair.

Parade magazine reported that skeptics were soon won over as Reese "moved her arms and spun her chair around, dancing in sync with the music. It was an unconventional routine but one she performed to near perfection."

Challes Reese won a spot on the dance squad. Later she performed in the annual Iowa State Dance and Drill Team Association competition.

It's important to have dreams and to encourage them in young people.

Do all that you have in mind, for God is with you. (1 Chronicles 17:2)

Keep me from limiting myself and hopes for the future, Holy God, by believing in Your faith in me.

Basketball Buddies

For the team at Omaha's Mercy High School, basketball is much more than fun and games.

The varsity girls mentor the fifth-grade team at Our Lady of Lourdes School. The program got started when the parochial school's new coach, Julia Brekel, asked Mercy High's Nicole Strongren for coaching tips. It grew into Basketball Buddies.

"Coach Strongren has taught her girls commitment, passion and values that help them on and off the court," said Brekel. "The really neat thing is to see these high school teenagers showing up at 8 a.m. games on a Saturday or spending their Friday nights hanging out with a fifth-grader."

The older girls appreciate their ability to influence others. The younger ones get important role models for sports—and life.

Youngsters need to be shown the ropes—or the hoops. Be generous with your time and talent.

Let no one despise your youth, but set the believers an example in speech and conduct, in love, in faith, in purity. (1 Timothy 4:12)

Inspire us to inspire others, gracious Lord. Let us know who needs what we have to give.

A Bronx Love Gospel

Over 200 devastated parishioners of the Love Gospel Assembly met in their church parking lot one July morning even as the smoke from a four-alarm fire hung over their heads. The 90-year-old building had sustained major damages from the blaze and had to be closed.

Yet those gathered were determined to rebuild. "Though the building may be shut down, we're not shut down," said Bishop Ronald L. Bailey, the senior pastor. "We live in a negative world, a negative environment, but we serve a positive God."

The church is closely tied to its struggling community and providing meals to more than 400 needy people a day. In a neighborhood where hope is a fragile thing, the congregation refuses to give up. In the words of one member, "our hope is in Christ...we don't put hope in a building."

Entrust your hopes and desires to God.

If we hope for what we do not see, we wait for it with patience. (Romans 8:25)

Eternal Lord, remind us that Your treasure lies not in any earthly structure but in the loving hearts of Your children.

Love Drives Out Hate

The Rev. Dr. Martin Luther King Jr. remains one of the most powerful and eloquent civil rights leaders in U.S. history. Here are just a few of his memorable statements:

- "Returning violence for violence multiplies violence, adding deeper darkness to a night already devoid of stars...Hate cannot drive out hate; only love can do that."
- "Let no man pull you low enough to hate him."
- "I believe that unarmed truth and unconditional love will have the final word in reality. That is why right, temporarily defeated, is stronger than evil triumphant."
- "Hatred paralyzes life; love releases it. Hatred confuses life; love harmonizes it. Hatred darkens life; love illuminates it."
- "The good neighbor looks beyond the external accidents and discerns those inner qualities that make all men human and, therefore, brothers."

When you come together...let all things be done for building up. (1 Corinthians 14:26)

Help us remember that every person we meet is also Your child, Father.

The Gift of Life

In his junior year at Rowan University, Matt Hoffman, a star football player for the school, donated his bone stem cells to a local marrow bank. In order to donate, Matt had to end his junior football season early so that he could take the necessary drugs to begin the extraction. He had to choose between a football game and saving a life. Matt chose life.

Matt's donation was a match for Warren Sallach, a cancer patient from Texas. With treatment from Matt's bone stem cells, Warren is now cancer free.

The donor from New Jersey and the patient from Texas met for the first time with their families. During the visit, words were hard to find for both men, especially for Warren who admitted, "There's nothing you can say except thank you and that doesn't cover it."

Praise God for your life and the lives of the people you love. Prayerfully consider visiting your local blood bank or marrow bank to make a donation.

For with You is the fountain of life; in Your light do we see light. (Psalm 36:9)

God of life, breathe in me Your very breath that I may give wholly of myself.

Understanding the Office Tyrant

There's a movement in offices to understand and defuse workplace bullies by examining their early psychology.

Psychologist Sylvia LaFair has identified 13 different patterns of office behavior—and the family dynamics that likely shaped them, including the persecutor, the denier and the martyr. LaFair recommends making simple observations without attacking, waiting for it to sink in, and listening carefully to the response. She also recommends asking questions to help your co-worker become conscious of how his or her bad behavior affects others.

Lars Dalgaard, chief executive of SuccessFactors, used to be brutally blunt with his subordinates. After he was confronted, he realized he was imitating his father's behavior by playing the macho CEO. Now Dalgaard fights old patterns by having his employees speak honestly about how his behavior affects their performance.

Think about how your actions affect others. Do your best to bring out the best in everyone.

**Love does no wrong to a neighbor.
(Romans 13:10)**

Holy Wisdom, fill us with understanding for the failures of others even as we confront our own, so that all grow wiser.

Unwrapping Hope

Annie felt helpless. She really wanted to be with her sister-in-law, Lauren, who was facing breast cancer surgery, but work prevented the 1,000-mile journey.

Then Annie had an idea. "Even though I can't be with you," she wrote in a note to Lauren, "I'm sending some things to surround you with love and beauty."

Annie wrapped up almost a dozen items to send with the note, offering Lauren the meaning of each.

There was, for example, a small figurine of an angel standing on her head to remind Lauren to tap into her playful spirit during recovery. A tiny ceramic tulip was enclosed to help her focus on the beauty often hidden in life's darkest moments. And four small duck-shaped soaps were designed to help Lauren connect with the loving hearts of Annie's grandchildren as well as her own nephews and niece.

Near or far, we can reach out in love and foster hope.

I am continually with you; You hold my right hand. (Psalm 73:23)

My spirit finds joy resting in Your love, Lord; You bring me peace.

An Undelivered Pizza Saves a Life

One of the virtues of developing a habit is that other people notice when you stop.

To be sure, Jean had a different kind of habit: she ate pizza every night for dinner. Not many people would call that virtuous.

But when she didn't order pizza for three days straight, Susan, her usual delivery person, noticed and went to Jean's house to check on her.

Nobody answered the door, so Susan talked to a neighbor who hadn't seen Jean either. Susan then called 911. The police found Jean on her floor inside the house.

It turns out she had fallen and couldn't get over to a telephone to call for help. Her pizza-only diet helped save her, as did her concerned delivery person.

In describing Jean, Susan said, "She treats us really well. She appreciates us, and that's something we don't get in customers a lot."

Treating others with kindness and respect is a virtuous habit worth developing. It might even save your life!

For I was hungry and you gave me food, I was thirsty and you gave me drink, a stranger and you welcomed me. (Matthew 25:35)

Lord, may we appreciate all the people in our life!

Kudos to Caregivers!

As the population of our country ages, the role of caregiver has become more prevalent for many people. Often, it's a job thrust upon an unprepared and already overworked loved one.

Here are some tips that may help caregivers cope with a demanding role and avoid neglecting their own well-being:

- Don't beat yourself up because you are not a perfect caregiver. After all, no one's perfect.
- Admit that the work you do is hard, demanding and stressful.
- Remember to take breaks—even small ones.
- Enjoy and relish as many joyful moments as you can with the person you're caring for.
- Pray. Ask God for strength when care-giving eclipses your own needs.

And, if you are not a caregiver yourself, be sure to support friends or relatives who are and could use your help.

Bear one another's burdens. (Galatians 6:2)

Infuse me with compassion for the suffering, Christ.

The Greatest Joy

Lacy Dodd experienced an unplanned pregnancy while a senior at Notre Dame in 1999. Despite being encouraged by some to have an abortion, she held to the faith and values that she saw modeled by her family throughout her life.

Lacy gave birth to her daughter and raised her as a single mother while serving in the Army for five years. She now works in corporate America in North Carolina and serves on the Board of Directors of the Charlotte-based pregnancy resource center Room at the Inn.

During an interview on the *Christopher Closeup* radio show/podcast, Lacy explained her involvement with the project. She said, "In today's world, too many women think they have to sacrifice their children for their education and career, but that's just not true. There are so many alternatives to abortion. I personally chose single parenting, and I've had rewarding careers in the military and now in corporate America. But what has given me the greatest joy in life is my child."

The Lord called me...in my mother's womb. (Isaiah 49:1)

Lord, help all expectant parents find the love and support they need.

Learning: It Never Goes Out of Style

Shirley Garrison is a college student who typically signs up for at least eight classes per semester. She's also a teacher of writing, a retiree, and 82 years of age.

Garrison is one of many senior-age retirees who have embraced the ongoing joy of learning. Her vehicle: The Lifelong Learning Institute, a program offered by Harper College in Illinois, where seniors over age 55 can experience the joy of learning through a slew of non-credit courses offered in an array of subjects.

The classes focus on learning and discussion, and do not include tests, textbooks, writing papers or even grades. "You just go in and enjoy it," she says. "It thrills me."

Garrison doesn't see the endeavor as work. "I can't imagine why anyone wouldn't want to keep their mind going like this," she says.

Perhaps we really are as young as we feel. Learning shouldn't have to stop because we reach a certain age.

How attractive is wisdom in the aged, and understanding and counsel. (Sirach 25:5)

Keep us youthful through our faith, Lamb of God.

Bring Cheer to Teens

According to a recent study, anxiety, depression and other mental-health issues are far more prevalent among youth today than during the Great Depression.

Why? Researchers speculate that modern society's emphasis on material wealth and external appearances as well as its standards of success and beauty have skewed young people's expectations.

"We have become a culture that focuses more on material things, and less on relationships," says psychologist Jean Twenge.

Other researchers suggest that overprotective parenting, which stunts kids' ability to develop coping skills, contributes to the problem. Whatever the causes, the picture is unsettling: On average, five times as many students in 2007 reported signs of mental illness than did those in 1938.

Make an effort to reach out to young people. Your efforts could influence a young life for the better.

My child, honor yourself with humility, and give yourself the esteem you deserve. (Sirach 10:28)

Protect our children, Lord Jesus, from illness of mind or body.

In a Single Moment

A single moment can change one's outlook.

Kate Goldrick of New Jersey writes of such a moment, an event she witnessed on an ordinary street during an ordinary day.

En route to work, Goldrick often saw a blind woman walking with her guide dog. One rainy morning, Goldrick saw the woman standing at the curb, trying to urge her dog to cross the street. The dog, however, would not cross: before them lay a large, deep puddle.

The blind woman seemed frustrated and confused. Finally, a man approached, saying, "Hello Ma'am. Your dog doesn't want to cross because there's a puddle. Take my hand and I'll help you cross and keep your feet dry."

Goldrick said of the event, "I actually teared up. It made my day to see such a kind gesture."

Acts of kindness reap riches for others and for ourselves. Be kind every day.

Does not a word surpass a good gift? Both are to be found in a gracious person. (Sirach 18:17)

Infuse us with a willingness to be hospitable to strangers, Holy Paraclete.

Doing More with Less

Some people wonder what help exists for those who are poor or newly unemployed. Soup kitchens, food pantries, detox programs and subsidized housing are helpful though inadequate.

"We want to be open every day, but my fear is with the economy the way it is, we'll run out of food in a few days and just be open once a week," said the director of one soup kitchen. "There is no bailout for us. There hasn't been one for years. The closest thing to a bailout for us is to do more with less."

Troubling stories abound. One family moved to a shelter after the father lost his job, but they lost food stamps after missing a required interview.

Stories of kindness also surface, like the out-of-work construction worker who donated baby clothes to a family even worse off.

Compassion should be as natural to us as breathing—because it's as necessary.

Cast all your anxiety on Him, because He cares for you. (1 Peter 5:7)

Jesus, Lord and Brother, steer me in the direction of love no matter what my own problems may be.

Community Connections

When Michael Wood-Lewis and his wife, Valerie, moved to Burlington, Vermont, they thought they'd landed in their dream neighborhood. There was only one catch: it seemed nearly impossible to connect with any of their neighbors.

One night, they realized that when they lived in other regions of the country, people brought cookies to their neighbors.

"Where were our cookies?" they wondered. So the couple baked up a batch of cookies and delivered them to the neighbors. "We used china plates, because I figured that way they'd have to return them and we'd get another conversation," jokes Wood-Lewis.

Then, Wood-Lewis created an online forum for the neighborhood. Ninety percent of the community signed up, and helped organize charity events, parties and efforts to help other neighbors in need.

Connect with your neighbors in positive ways.

Do not neglect to show hospitality...by doing that, some have entertained angels without knowing it. (Hebrews 13:2)

Unite our communities in looking out for each and every neighbor, Holy Redeemer.

Is There a Musician in the House?

In 1999, there was a concert at the Memorial Sloan-Kettering Cancer Center in New York City. Nurses carefully transported patients to the hospital's recreation area, arranging seats and wheelchairs around a temporary stage. As the music played, feet tapped, heads nodded to the beat, and smiles formed on faces.

It was just what the patients needed, one nurse said, but what a shame those unable to leave their rooms couldn't have the experience.

So that day, Musicians On Call was born. After finishing the concert, musicians left the stage to play at the bedsides of those who couldn't leave their rooms. Since then, volunteer musicians have performed for more than 250,000 patients and their families at health-care facilities in New York, as well as in Nashville, Philadelphia and Miami.

In our darkest moments, we must trust that hope will find us.

With trumpets and the sound of the horn, make a joyful noise before the King, the Lord. (Psalm 98:6)

Strengthen me, Lord, that I may share Your love and hope this day.

Small Beginning, Big Ending

It started out as a trip to Guasmo Sur, Ecuador, to show charitable donors where their donations were being put to work. Msgr. Raymond Kirk, pastor of a San Diego parish, organized it so they could learn more about how their generosity translated into aid for the needy.

Among the travelers were Katie Brown and Betty Matteson. "It was a real eye-opener," says Matteson. Both women say that visit laid the groundwork for their ongoing project, Friends of Hospital Madre Berenice, or FHMB. It's a non-profit organization that supports Guasmo Sur's hospital by raising money for needs such as X-ray equipment, incubators and medical supplies.

Says Brown, "We're all called to be missionaries. Some are called to go to the missions, and others are called to support the missions."

Good works come in many forms. Find a creative way to alleviate the suffering of the needy and the sick.

I led them with cords of human kindness, with bands of love...I bent down to them and fed them. (Hosea 11:4)

Have mercy on the suffering, the hungry, the imprisoned, Merciful Savior.

Hats Off — and On — to Our Troops

JoAnne Schottler of Stratham, New Hampshire, wanted to express her gratitude to the men and women who serve on active military duty in Iraq and Afghanistan. So she organized volunteers who crochet hats for the troops to wear under their helmets.

The volunteers have distributed over 5,000 hats and have more ready to be placed on each seat aboard the chartered flights that carry troops from Portsmouth International Airport to the Middle East.

"Never in my wildest dreams did I think this program would fly like this," says Schottler of their effort.

Gail Curran, a volunteer, adds a special message to the hats she makes: "I write that there's a prayer for them in every stitch."

Show respect for our troops and for veterans, regardless of your opinions about war or politics. And encourage others, especially young people, to do the same.

Whenever we have an opportunity, let us work for the good of all. (Galatians 6:10)

Watch over our troops and their families, Savior. And reunite them in Your peace.

Ask...and You Shall Receive, In Abundance

Fran Karoff was surfing the Internet to find an affordable piano for her young son. "I was looking for a used piano so my seven-year-old son could learn to play," she says. She found a Victorian model and called the owner.

The two connected and had a friendly conversation. Much to Karoff's surprise, the owner decided right then and there to give the piano to her—for free. The owner said that Karoff "wanted the piano for all the right reasons."

As if this weren't generous enough, the owner insisted on paying all shipping costs. "Needless to say I was extremely touched by her kindness and will always be grateful," says Karoff.

An act of kindness is more complete when the recipient graciously accepts—and appreciates—the generosity of another. Accept gifts with grace and remember that expressing appreciation completes another's act of kindness.

Be rich in good works, generous, and ready to share. (1 Timothy 6:18)

Holy Spirit, enable me to accept love as well as to offer it.

Small Steps and Little Victories

Madieu Williams came to the U.S. from Sierra Leone, Africa, when he was only 9 years old. Now, a successful football player with the NFL's Minnesota Vikings, he returns to Sierra Leone each year to visit the school he opened in 2008.

The Abigail D. Butscher Primary School is named in memory of Madieu's mother, who was a nurse. Though she died at the young age of 45, Madieu is keeping her memory alive by supporting the school of 150 students, which he hopes to expand.

He also donated two million dollars to his alma mater, the University of Maryland, to fund education and health care research that will help places like Sierra Leone.

Madieu reminds people, "Take small steps. Small successes are good when there's a huge problem. You try to focus on the little victories."

Do you see a need within your community or even abroad where God is calling you to help? What small steps can you take?

Thus says the Lord: Maintain justice, and do what is right, for soon My salvation will come, and My deliverance be revealed. (Isaiah 56:1)

Embolden us, Father, with the courage to fight injustice.

Most Valuable Coach

When Wake Forest University freshman Kevin Jordan needed a kidney transplant, none of his family members were a suitable match for a donation.

Kevin had recently been diagnosed with ANCA vasculitis, which left his kidneys functioning at eight percent. His first semester included daily dialysis.

Upon learning that none of Kevin's family members were a match, Tom Walter—his college baseball coach—decided to get tested too, despite the fact that Kevin hadn't even played for him yet. Coach Walter was a match, and became the donor.

His baseball team wasn't surprised. One senior outfielder said "[Coach] is a very stand-up man at all times. When he made a commitment to Kevin, he did it for good and bad. That's just the type of guy he is."

Kevin's family knows God's hand is in this, and is beyond grateful. Coach Walter is more nonchalant about his contribution. He says, "If [Kevin] makes it back to the playing field, that would be a great story. I just want him to have a normal life."

This I command you: love one another. (John 15:17)

Lord, give us the courage to follow Your example.

Uncomplicating Compliments

From an early age, we are socialized to believe that complimenting is a straightforward and essential part of human interaction.

Yet as we age, we recognize that "there's a fine art to giving—and receiving—a well-tailored compliment," writes Elizabeth Bernstein. The pressure we feel to give and receive compliments graciously can be a source of social anxiety. How can we ease our tension and that of others? Here are some ideas:

- We hear what we want to hear. When we're mired in self-doubt we can misunderstand. Learn to listen clearly.
- We often disregard the praise of those closest to us. Appreciate the sentiment before judging the source.
- Be selective, sincere, and specific. Not too big or too small, just right.
- Just say thank you! Graciousness comes with practice.

Give thanks in all circumstances, for this is the will of God in Christ Jesus for you.
(1 Thessalonians 5:18)

God of Love, grant courage and patience to us and to others as we continually learn how to share this world.

The Cost of Discipleship

One of the winning books honored during the 2011 Christopher Awards ceremony was Eric Metaxas' biography *Bonhoeffer: Pastor, Martyr, Prophet, Spy.*

Faced with Nazi policies that subverted core Christian beliefs, Lutheran pastor Dietrich Bonhoeffer called on his fellow Germans to defend the Jewish people.

When most didn't, he attributed their silence to "cheap grace"—the notion that you could be authentically Christian without enduring sacrifice to follow the gospel.

Metaxas' riveting biography explores Bonhoeffer's life, theology, and moral dilemmas—from his insights on the proper relationship between church and state, to his working as a double agent to save Jewish lives.

Eventually executed for his role in a plot to overthrow Hitler, Bonhoeffer faced death peacefully, having accepted it as the cost of true Christian discipleship.

Pray for the courage to not stay silent in the face of evil.

You guide me with Your counsel, and afterward You will receive me with honor. (Psalm 73:24)

Help us live according to Your values, Lord.

Turning Deprivation Into Innovation

An award-winning inventor at the Massachusetts Institute of Technology (MIT), José Gómez-Márquez attributes much of his admiration—and understanding—of all things technical to his impoverished beginnings in his native Honduras.

"When you grow up in a developing country, you get the sense that fancy technology is expensive to replace," he says. Not surprisingly, Gómez-Márquez today creates and refines instruments and equipment for doctors in poor countries where expensive part replacements are impossible to obtain. He uses everything from toy parts, common household items and tools to make functional, low-cost medical devices.

For example, he is currently creating an "erector set" that will enable doctors in poor regions to devise diagnostics, drug delivery devices and more.

How can you channel your unique talents to help others?

I have given you an example that by such work we must support the weak, remembering the words of the Lord Jesus, for He Himself said, "It is more blessed to give than to receive." (Acts 20:35)

Inspire me to bring forth new creations, Gracious Father.

A Civil Rights Legacy

When we think of great civil rights leaders, the name Jonathan Walker may not leap to mind. But Walker was an extraordinarily courageous champion of the abolitionist movement in 1800s America.

Born in 1799, Walker was a happily married father, a seaman by trade and a devout Christian. He abhorred slavery and helped runaway slaves from Florida by taking them on board his ship to sail to the Bahamas, where blacks were free.

The ship, however, was stopped by Florida authorities, and Walker was imprisoned. He suffered a red-hot branding iron upon his hand as part of his punishment.

Rather than hide his scar, Walker brandished it as an honor. After the Emancipation Proclamation, Walker spent the rest of his life fighting for justice and equality for all black Americans.

Good deeds, however hidden, do not escape the eyes of God. Work for justice and you will reap bountiful rewards!

Commit your ways to the Lord; trust in Him and He will act. He will make your vindication shine like the light, and the justice of your cause like the noonday. (Psalm 37:5-6)

Recognize and reward the brave who seek justice, Father.

Sledding: A Rich History

For those who grew up in an area that had four seasons, sledding is likely a fond childhood memory.

Writer Catherine Riedel describes her sledding remembrances: "Your mother lovingly bundling you into your snowsuit; tingling cheeks, a runny nose, glints of sunlight, crunchy snow underfoot; then an exhilarating whoosh, bump, bounce; followed by a long, graceful glide."

In America, the activity is firmly planted in our history. While sledding was a frequent, though makeshift activity in the colonies in the 1600s and 1700s, by the 1840s, downhill coasting sleds were being built for recreation. By 1861, sled racing had caught on as a sport, and sleds were being mass-produced and widely marketed throughout the country.

What memories do you hold dear from your childhood? How can you help create a lasting happy memory for a child?

Let the little children come to Me...for it is to such as these the Kingdom of Heaven belongs. (Matthew 19:14)

Shelter Your little ones from harm, Heavenly Father.

The Bible in the Boardroom?

A growing trend suggests more and more workers are bringing their creeds to their cubicles.

According to David Miller, author of *God at Work: The History and Promise of the Faith at Work Movement,* there's been a marked shift in attitudes toward what he calls the workplace's final taboo: spirituality and religion. As a result, there's been a rise in faith-based employee networks, lunchtime prayer meetings, Bible groups and e-mail lists that send scripture out over company servers. What's more, the trend runs across denominations.

Elaine Kung, who participates in a weekly Bible study group at her office, says, "God is a 24-by-7 God, not just once in a weekend."

Some say a disconnect between one's work and faith is harmful. Others believe religion is best left outside the office. Where do you stand?

All scripture is inspired by God and is useful for teaching, for reproof, for correction, and for training in righteousness. (2 Timothy 3:16-17)

Inspire my work so that I may fulfill my mission, Divine Master.

Seeing is Believing

Love is a universal language understood by all of God's creatures, big and small.

Having limited sight in one of his eyes, Graham Waspe of Suffolk, England, obtained a yellow Labrador named Edward from the Guide Dogs Charity in 2004. After six years of service, Edward had to have his own eyes removed due to cataracts.

Soon after this unfortunate event, a two-year-old female guide dog named Opal arrived on the scene, ready and willing to help both Waspe and her predecessor. Not only does she serve as a guide for Graham and Edward, she also proved to be an invaluable playmate and friend.

And though Edward may have lost his sight, he did not lose his ability to play or love. This winsome threesome has grown quite popular around the neighborhood, frequently visiting schools and participating in fundraising events.

In his infinite compassion and mercy, God will never leave you completely in the dark.

Your word is a lamp to my feet, and a light to my path. (Psalm 119:105)

Dear Lord, help to shine light into those whose lives are cloaked in darkness.

Using Art to Teach History

"I was surprised at how many things in one painting can be significant," said Michael Maxwell. "What the subjects are holding. What they are wearing. The position they are in the painting and who is with them."

As a high school student in Omaha, Maxwell has come to appreciate art through a church history class taught by Mattie Germer. After a trip to Italy, the teacher incorporated more visual elements into classes.

"I was trying to find ways to make things stick," she said. "Coupled with the fact that we live in a very visual culture, I thought this is a way that I can make these stories from church history more meaningful."

Maxwell has certainly learned a great deal. "Everything painted or drawn has a meaning," the teen says. "Nothing is painted accidentally."

And every individual life has meaning as well.

He carved the walls of the house all around about with carved engravings of cherubim, palm trees, and open flowers. (1 Kings 6:29)

Holy Paraclete, open our eyes to the beauty around us, especially the beauty of Your love for us.

To Sleep, Perchance to Breathe

Catching the annual common cold is no fun for any of us. Sneezing, congestion, achiness and fatigue are not synonymous with productivity, work or, especially, having fun.

Yet the common cold is largely unavoidable for most of us, a daunting fate when we consider the impact a cold can have on our lives.

According to the *New York Post,* colds account for 100 million trips to the doctor, 1.5 million emergency-room visits, hundreds of millions of work absences and 189 million absences from school. So why can't scientists find a way to cure it?

Perhaps the reason scientists and researchers remain stumped lies in the cold virus itself. Small enough for 50,000 of them to fit on the head of a pin, no two cold viruses are alike. Also, some of us are genetically more disposed to catching colds than others.

Until the mystery is solved, bundle up, drink plenty of fluids and get some rest!

For I will restore health to you, and your wounds will I heal, says the Lord. (Jeremiah 30:17)

Honor those who seek to cure and comfort the sick.

Sacrilegious or Sacred?

Father Ronald Raab and members of his Portland, Oregon, parish initially didn't appreciate Bonnie, a local "bag lady."

Bonnie went to their hospitality center "in search of new clothing and a warm breakfast. Her boundless energy disturbed everyone's routine," wrote Father Raab in *U.S. Catholic*. "We panicked as she stuffed food into her pockets, paperback novels under her jacket, and rolls of toilet paper in her plastic bag."

Although she used her "penetrating voice" at inopportune moments, eventually Father Raab viewed her differently. Bonnie and others "marginalized by poverty or mental illness needed to be *heard*," said Father Raab. He interpreted her disturbing words and actions as a wake-up call.

We need to speak up for those whose suffering—whether due to disease, poverty or loneliness—is hidden or ignored.

We declare to you what was from the beginning, what we have heard...concerning the word of life. (1 John 1:1)

Let us hear those in need or in trouble, Blessed Trinity.

Healing in a Box

Sadie was feeling defeated. Her high blood pressure, life-threatening without her medication, seemed these days to be more than she could handle.

On this particular day at work, she was searching through her office for something a colleague had asked her to find. In one drawer, she found instead a small white box with a handwritten note on top from her daughter.

"To Mom," it read, "I love you and I think you need this angel the most." The gift inside—from a Mother's Day of the past—was a small charm, with an angel on one side and the word "healing" on the other.

Suddenly, Sadie felt lighter—healed immediately in spirit and in body as well.

We are never really alone in our sufferings. Family and friends—and through them, the Lord Himself—are there to make life's burdens and difficulties easier to carry.

But rejoice insofar as you are sharing God's sufferings, so that you may also be glad...when His glory is revealed. (1 Peter 4:13)

I put my faith in You, Lord, and trust in Your love.

The Safe Haven of Commitment

With the success of books and movies like *The Notebook* and *Dear John*, Nicholas Sparks has a well-founded reputation for being able to craft romantic stories that touch people's hearts.

But romance alone isn't enough to create a meaningful, lasting relationship like he's had with his wife Cathy for over twenty years.

On The Christophers' radio show/podcast *Christopher Closeup*, Sparks explained that he once had a debate with his brother, Micah, about this very topic.

Micah suggested that communication is most important in a relationship. That led Nicholas to ask, "What does communication matter if you're not committed to each other? People who've been married a long time know that emotionally, it's going to go up and down. If you're committed, you know you'll work through whatever's keeping you down, that you'll come out on the other side, and it will get better again."

If your marriage is facing hard times, acknowledge the problem, stay committed and seek help.

As I have loved you, you also should love one another. (John 13:34)

Thank you for Your commitment to loving me, Lord.

Sharing the Shirts Off Their Backs

Zoe Baris volunteered at a clothing drive with her mom. She learned there were no such projects for young people, and so she started one.

The Cleveland, Ohio, teen asked her friend Samantha Zabell to join her. Together they co-founded Share What You Wear. The pair accepts donations year-round, storing the clothing, shoes and accessories in Zoe's basement. They use monetary contributions to purchase new underwear and socks.

Working with local social service and foster care agencies, they identify needy families and distribute the merchandise.

As Zoe and Samantha head off to college, they plan to help establish similar ventures near their respective campuses. "There are people in need everywhere," says Zoe. "And there are teens willing to help."

There are "calls to action" surrounding us every day. How will you respond to someone's needs today?

I was naked and you gave me clothing. (Matthew 25:36)

Strengthen me, Lord, that I may better love my neighbor.

A Letter From Sister

Sister Mary Mark Mahoney taught elementary school for more than 35 years, and even helped start a house of prayer.

But the 100-year-old Religious Sister from Minnesota will tell you that writing to death row inmates for the past 16 years is "the best thing I ever did."

"I don't ask what they did," Sister Mary Mark explains. Nor does she condone their actions.

"I let them know that we are all God's children," she says, "and I remind them that God loves us no matter what."

Sister Mary Mark suspects that most on death row have nobody communicating with them. "So somebody who takes the time to communicate with somebody like that will be, I think, rewarded in heaven," she adds.

In our own lives, we need to remember that our Lord's love is for all people—including those we may judge unworthy.

Beloved, let us love one another. (1 John 4:7)

Forgive me the wrong I do, Father, as I forgive my neighbor.

The Friendly Cabby

Many people imagine New York City cab drivers as reckless, impulsive drivers caring little about their passengers. Just don't let Rafael Crichlow hear that.

Crichlow, a cab driver, recently won recognition as the city's Friendliest Driver at the annual awards ceremony, held by the Taxi and Limousine Commission. He earned rave reviews from passengers, particularly a handicapped woman whom he helped descend from his taxi. "That's the way I was raised," Crichlow said.

And his story was only one of many. Rachid Rakhis won the Good Samaritan prize for reporting a potentially dangerous passenger to the police. Mamarame Ndiaye took home an award for safe driving, having gone over three years without an accident.

You never need to look hard to find exceptions to common stereotypes. Keep this in mind when you meet others. Take each person you meet as they are, not as you imagine them to be.

Whoever belittles another lacks sense, but an intelligent person remains silent.
(Proverbs 11:12)

Creator of All, remind me to reject prejudices and stereotypes and see each person as a unique individual.

A World of Ideas

A World Science Festival held in New York City showcased the creative talents of several inventors.

One of them, Diana Eng, designs clothing that combines fashion and technology. One of her recent projects is a hooded sweatshirt that monitors the wearer's heartbeat and, as that increases, a tiny camera takes a photo. "You'll end up with photos at the end of the day of the things that stimulated your heart," Eng said.

Former advertising executive Patrick Raymond invented something called the ShowerBow to keep shower curtains from blowing around. He said it wasn't a flash of genius: "really more like a flash of annoyance that leads to someone trying to solve a problem in a new and unique way."

Another creator said she'd never invented before but had an inventive mind. "I like to figure things out and problem-solve."

Nurture your God-given creativity.

Each has a particular gift from God, one having one kind and another a different kind. (1 Corinthians 7:7)

You give each of us so many talents and abilities, Lord. Help me to use mine to benefit Your people.

Inspired by Faith and Fatherhood

When screenwriter and children's author Frank Cottrell Boyce was asked how his faith affected his work, he responded, "In every single way, I think."

Boyce tries to reinforce the idea that, "Life is amazing, and the world is a phenomenally wonderful place and full of grace."

He cites fatherhood as his main impetus for spreading this message in his writing, claiming: "People are selling a lot of fake happiness to our children. You know what real happiness is? It's the day we did this together, the day we played in the sun together, those little tiny pleasures that families share."

When asked how he wished to be remembered as a writer, Boyce replied, "I'd like to be remembered as a dad."

How do you wish to be remembered?

The memory of the righteous is a blessing. (Proverbs 10:7)

Help us to bring light to the darkness in our world with our loving words and actions, Merciful Father.

A Life Without Freedom

Imagine not being able to celebrate or even observe your religious or spiritual beliefs. That's how Deacon Bohdan Hedz, of St. John the Baptist Ukrainian Church in Syracuse, New York, grew up in Western Ukraine.

While his nation was under Communist rule, religious observances, whether holidays, traditions or practices, were forbidden or, at best, strictly controlled. Hedz's parents had to have him baptized in secret.

Now that he's in the United States, Deacon Hedz guards religious freedom zealously. "People take their faith for granted here," he observes. "Nobody oppressed you, nobody took away your church."

Since Communist rule was ended in 1991, Ukrainian Catholics and others have been able to worship without fear.

Give thanks for all of the freedoms with which Americans have been so richly blessed. Do all you can to preserve them.

Happy is the nation whose God is Lord. (Psalm 33:12)

May our nation remain faithful and free, Gracious Father.

Swimming for School

As cold weather envelops areas in winter months, it's not unusual to see groups clad in swimsuits head for icy waters in defiance of nature.

The polar plungers may just be challenging the elements—or, perhaps, raising money for worthy causes.

Such was the case one recent winter day along the New Jersey shore when more than 400 hardy souls of all ages—led by a local Catholic bishop—dunked into the frigid deep, backed by others who had pledged cash if they did so.

Money raised that day—a record-breaking total of $102,000—supported some 20 Catholic schools.

"It's all about friendship and unity and Christian charity," offered one participant.

Any action, motivated by our love of neighbor, can bring warmth and joy to life's sometimes cold, harsh reality.

May the God of steadfastness and endurance grant you to live in harmony with one another. (Romans 15:5)

When life's difficulties wash over me, I look to You, Lord, for rescue and relief.

40 Days for Life

Beginning in Texas in 2004, the 40 Days for Life campaign "has proven life-saving results," said David Berent, national director. Pro-life advocates spend the time from Ash Wednesday to Palm Sunday focusing on prayer, fasting and outreach. Hundreds of communities around the U.S.A. have participated over the years.

The 40-day period is taken from examples throughout biblical history in which God created transformations within people and the world itself in that time-frame. Supporters concentrate their efforts on opening hearts and minds to alternatives to abortion.

In one community, participants included men from the local correctional facility who contributed to the vigil through prayer and fasting. Other activists provided educational information about pregnancy and health-care decisions.

Do all you can to affirm life and to encourage others to do the same.

With prayer and fasting they entrusted them to the Lord in whom they had come to believe. (Acts 14:23)

Creator of all, bless Your people and guide us as we seek to respect life from conception to death.

A Complaint-Free World

Emma Wescott, an Albany, New York, native, is among millions doing it—or rather, not doing it. Complaining, that is.

Both she and her husband, Joseph, have joined A Complaint-Free World, a movement to ditch negative thoughts and become more positive, hopeful and optimistic.

It started with Will Bowen, a Protestant minister, who suggested that his Missouri congregation wear purple bracelets as a visual reminder to turn off negativity. Today more than six million bracelets have been sent to 106 countries across the globe.

Each day without complaint, criticism or gossip is counted. The bracelet is shifted to the other wrist when one occurs, and the count begins again. "It's really changed the way I look at things, and feel about things," Joseph says.

With a positive spirit, life's everyday moments—even the rough ones—will be made that much easier.

Do all things without murmuring...so that you may be blameless and innocent, children of God. (Philippians 2:14-15)

May a spirit of joy guide my thoughts and actions this day, Lord.

Find Quiet Time

Most people love to talk or let others know what they are thinking. So they make phone calls, send text messages, leave Facebook posts, maybe even call in to talk radio programs. It's the other side of the equation, listening, that seems less appealing.

Yet listening holds the key to unlocking ourselves and our place in God's plan. Pope Benedict XVI, speaking at a Lenten retreat, says that only by listening "can one know oneself," that to fulfill our potential, we must "listen to others and especially to God."

Only when we sit still can we hear God's voice. So turn off your cell phone. Ignore your e-mail. Take time each day for quiet reflection. And in the silence, listen. God will speak to you.

When you are disturbed, do not sin; ponder it on your beds and be silent. (Psalm 4:4)

Holy Spirit, remind me to take the time each day to stop and listen to Your voice—and the voice of Your children as well.

National Treasures on Ice

Have you ever enjoyed America's national parks in winter?

For those who visit Yellowstone National Park then, the experience is different from that of the more customary summer tourists. That unique experience is one of the appeals of winter trips for Esther Bly—even though friends think she's crazy for leaving Florida's warmth for Wyoming's frigid weather.

The rewards of a winter visit include fewer crowds, less expensive rates, a blazing fire in the lodge fireplace, and a better chance to see wildlife such as bighorn sheep, bison, elk, moose, and possibly, the elusive wolf.

"Some of the best wildlife viewing is in winter," says a park official. "It's as simple as the color contrast. You can see the animals against the snow. It's almost a secret park. Different landscape. Different sounds. Different light."

National parks are truly a treasure to be appreciated whatever time of year.

As long as the earth endures, seedtime and harvest, cold and heat, summer and winter, day and night shall not cease. (Genesis 8:22)

Thank You for the beauty of our world, Almighty God. Help us to treat it wisely.

Life Isn't All Sunshine and Lollipops

Actress Patricia Heaton is well-known for playing a wife and Mom who makes us laugh on the TV series *Everybody Loves Raymond* and *The Middle*. But it was a tragedy involving her own mother that shaped the Emmy Award winner's life at an early age.

When Heaton was 12, her mother died suddenly of a brain aneurysm. The resulting emotional and spiritual struggle lasted for years, but Heaton credits her religious upbringing with helping her achieve a level of acceptance and peace.

As a guest on our *Christopher Closeup* radio show/podcast, she told program host Tony Rossi, "Rain will come into your life. You need to know that God is still there with you despite those problems...The life of a Christian doesn't guarantee sunshine and lollipops. I think once you let go of that idea—that if you become a Christian and follow God's will, your life is going to be a bed of roses—if you get past that, then you'll do okay."

Remember that God is walking with you—and sometimes even carrying you—through all of life's storms.

I am your God, I will strengthen you, I will help you. (Isaiah 41:10)

Lord, help me carry my cross today.

Barber Bounces Back

Sixty-four-year-old Bob Schlick's left leg was amputated below the knee after a debilitating motorcycle accident in 2008.

As if that weren't enough to worry about, Schlick was also concerned about the fate of his barbershop, Pacwest Hair Design, which he ran by himself in Portland, Oregon. It would take Bob several months to recover and he feared his customers would leave him before then. How wrong he was!

Prompted by his wife, customers started sending him letters, offering him boundless encouragement and wishes for a speedy recovery. Best of all, fellow Portland barber Allan Cooper offered to sell his own shop and partner with Schlick. He was soon joined by another barber, Allysha Johnson.

Eventually Schlick himself returned, happily cutting his clients' hair while sitting down. Though it will take time to obtain a prosthetic leg, he says, "I've never been happier."

Rejoice in what God has given you and trust him to take care of you when you are most in need.

Create in me a clean heart, O God, and put a new and right spirit within me. (Psalm 51:10)

Dear God, help me to recover from my losses in life and to give thanks for all the blessings You send me.

Your Brain Can Keep Growing

Can your brain improve with age? Barbara Strauch, in her book *The Secret Life of the Grown-up Brain,* says that the middle-aged brain is a contradiction. "Despite a misstep now and then, cognitive abilities continue to grow."

Neuroscientists believe that we can help ourselves by reading, exercising, eating well and staying involved with those around us and the world at large. They also expect continued scientific innovations which may help the human brain to function well through old age.

However, we still must overcome misinformation and stereotyping concerning the middle-aged and older brain. Strauch says, "The study of middle age is so new, as one scientist told me, 'It's like researching nuclear physics, something that simply did not exist before.'"

Undoubtedly science will learn more about the adult brain. In the meantime, do what you can for as long as you can.

Let the same mind be in you that was in Christ Jesus. (Philippians 2:5)

Holy Wisdom, guide my life at every stage and help me to serve You with my whole being.

Generosity Transforms a Life

After teenager Orayne Williams had been abandoned by his family, he found himself living in a Brooklyn, New York, homeless shelter. In some respects, the shelter was at least a respite from the abusive environment he endured while at home.

By the time he reached age 18, he was still living in the shelter. However, he excelled at school, maintaining a 91 average at Bedford Academy in Brooklyn's rough-and-tumble Bedford-Stuyvesant neighborhood.

The *New York Daily News* ran a story about him, and in the article's wake, more than $15,000 in donations poured in from readers. Soon after that, Manhattanville College in Purchase, New York, offered Williams admission on full scholarship, including his living expenses. "I was speechless," says Williams.

Generosity can change lives. Give of your time, talent and resources to the best of your ability.

Give and it will be given to you. (Luke 6:38)

Open our hearts so we give without hesitation, Father God.

Right Place, Right Time

Christopher Wuebben, a 22-year-old paramedic, decided to take a sabbatical from his job to serve as an EMT in Iraq. The experience left him well qualified to compete for most paramedic positions.

When he returned from his tour of duty, however, he found he'd been laid off. He couldn't find work. He even moved to another state to better his prospects, but could find nothing in his field. He resorted to pizza delivery to make ends meet.

While delivering a pizza to a residence, Wuebben discovered that a customer in the home had collapsed. "I'm a paramedic," he told the victim's wife, and proceeded to revive the man through CPR. Not long after, this "pizza guy" received several offers from local hospitals and fire departments, eager to hire him.

In humility, there is strength and even opportunity. We never know what lies behind the doors God puts before us, do we?

For surely I know the plans I have for you, says the Lord, plans...to give you a future with hope. (Jeremiah 29:11)

Enlighten me to see opportunity in struggle, Father God.

Children: The New Endangered Species?

Reverend Jemima Amanor, Director of Compassion International Ghana (CIG), has seen the harsh realities and repercussions of child abuse and neglect.

Abuses suffered by children around the globe include prostitution, trafficking, and child labor. Rev. Amanor believes that "it is these very children who are neglected who become armed robbers or terrorists." She adds that without a personal touch, youngsters can never develop the humanity that enables love.

CIG, a non-profit Christian ministry for children, was founded in 1952, and currently has more than one million children in 26 countries registered. It aims to provide financial and technical support to church partners for child development programs.

Many such committed organizations—and the individuals who enable their work—are essential if we want to give the children of the world hope for the future.

Depart from evil, and do good; seek peace, and pursue it. (Psalm 34:14)

Dear Lord, let us always be mindful that there is much we can do to help create Your peace on earth.

Volunteering Did the Trick

Heather Lodini had just turned 25 when she moved to Cromwell, Connecticut, and began a new job. "All the changes made me look at my life and I decided I needed to do something to feel more fulfilled," she recalls.

Lodini ran a half-marathon. She remodeled her kitchen. "I still didn't feel satisfied," she said. Then she became a volunteer, coaching those preparing for the Special Olympics.

The personal payoff has been huge. "I'm brought to tears when I see the look of joy in my athletes' faces."

Lodini subscribes to a "no excuses" philosophy since she began volunteering. "I've seen the challenges that people with disabilities face, so don't tell me that giving up a Saturday morning is hard," she says. "Life shouldn't be about us all the time."

Helping others is the best way to help yourself.

Like good stewards of the manifold grace of God, serve one another with whatever gift each of you has received. (1 Peter 4:10)

Steer us away from selfishness, Lord Jesus.

The Greatest of These...

When life treats us harshly, it helps to seek the guidance of those who have experienced difficulty in their own lives and yet continue to believe in goodness.

Archbishop Desmond Tutu is one such person. His fight for justice during South Africa's apartheid and into the present day has brought him face to face with the worst of human nature. Yet the renowned religious leader has kept his faith. In a *Time* magazine interview, Archbishop Tutu mused on how and why to believe, even in the darkest times:

"I'm not optimistic, no. I'm quite different. I'm hopeful. I am a prisoner of hope. ...Doubts? No. Anger with God? Yes. Plenty of that. I've remonstrated with God quite frequently and said, 'What the heck are you up to? Why are you letting these oppressors get away with this injustice?' But doubting that God is good? That God is love? No."

Open your heart to the vast, limitless love of God.

Trust in the Lord with all your heart. (Proverbs 3:5)

Holy Spirit, find us at our weakest and remind us of the unshakeable power of Your Love.

A Rising Star Reaches Out

Not everyone gets inspired to make a difference by their dentist, but that's what happened to former *American Idol* contestant David Archuleta.

The young singer's dentist had gotten involved with a charity called Rising Star Outreach which helps lepers in India. He encouraged his patient to learn more about their work.

When Archuleta went to the group's web site, he read stories of children and families cast out of villages because they were afflicted with leprosy and told they were cursed.

On The Christophers' radio show/podcast *Christopher Closeup*, Archuleta admitted his heart broke for these families. "It was hard," he said, "to see some of these people who are living the way they're living because of not having anyone there to care for them or want to be with them."

Believing this was a great cause to which he could lend his name, Archuleta has performed and spoken on Rising Star Outreach's behalf, and been impressed by how willing his fans are to help.

You don't have to be famous to make a difference. Reach out to someone in need.

Rescue the oppressed. (Isaiah 1:17)

God, make me generous and gracious.

No Job Too Small For Her

Sharon "Guppy" Litchfield has made a life out of serving the poor. It started with a simple request from her parish priest. "If anyone comes to the door [of the church], make them a big sandwich," was her charge.

From that, Litchfield ended up serving meals to 300 to 600 needy per day at Sacred Heart Church in Peoria, Illinois. "The program expanded—a lot," she jokes.

After years of serving in this program, Litchfield decided to move on. Her interaction with the parish priests, she says, always led to new opportunities for work.

"When one job ends, the Lord sends another," she says. However, the nature of her work—service—never changed. She's worked as a handyperson, ironed clothes, swept floors and cleaned toilets, work she regards as "peaceful."

Hard work not only doesn't daunt her, she revels in it. "If you don't give until it hurts, then it doesn't count," she says.

Speak out and judge righteously, defend the rights of the poor and needy. (Psalm 31:9)

Jesus, steer us toward a life of service.

5 Steps to a Better You

According to actress, working mother and "The Biggest Loser" host Alison Sweeney, there are five key steps to becoming "a better you."

1. Be committed. Whether you're looking to make a positive life change or even improve at something you already do, be willing to put in the time to succeed.

2. Be willing to learn from your mistakes. Sweeney once missed her cue to enter onstage at a performance. Today, she is "100 percent present" in her acting work.

3. Be yourself. If you want to change something in your life, do it for yourself, not because others feel you should.

4. Be balanced. Being a mother helped Alison Sweeney understand how to juggle her priorities. Follow her example—"take it one day at a time" and try not to sweat the small stuff!

5. Be prepared. As Sweeney says, "Study, practice, visualize and pray...so when an opportunity arises, you can grab it with both hands!"

A better you is possible. Just have faith in God and your own ability.

I can do all things through Him who strengthens me. (Philippians 4:13)

God, help me to create positive change in my life.

Doing the Right Thing

The tiny apartment of octogenarian Dr. Tina Strobos in Rye, New York, is filled with awards from a variety of Jewish organizations for her valiant work during the German occupation of the Netherlands in World War II.

She and her mother hid more than 100 Jews who passed through their rooming house in Amsterdam.

Dr. Strobos, who is not Jewish, recalls carrying news and ration stamps by bicycle, usually at great risk to her own life, to Jews hidden in various locations. At times, she was questioned and physically battered by the Gestapo in the process.

People have asked why she would take such a gamble for others, some of whom she hardly knew. "It was the right thing to do," she says.

Do "the right thing" always, regardless of the cost to you!

Deal courageously. (2 Chronicles 19:11)

Embolden us with the virtue of courage, Holy Paraclete.

From Grief, a Lifesaving Gift

Stacey Oglesby thought she'd never get over losing her 15-year-old daughter, Colbey, to a car accident. The grief was unbearable.

Colbey had told her mother that when she got her driver's license, she was going to sign up to be an organ donor. Colbey never got the chance to sign up. But upon her death, when hospital personnel asked Oglesby about organ donation, she says, "We had no hesitancy."

Seven people ended up receiving an organ from Colbey, including Valerie Vandervort, a young Oklahoma woman with cystic fibrosis, whose life was saved by the 15-year-old's lungs.

Oglesby has inspired others to become potential organ donors. If not for donating her daughter's organs, "It would have been hard to get through the grief."

Organ donation is a way to leave a lasting legacy of joy and life to others.

Precious in the sight of the Lord is the death of His faithful ones. (Psalm 116:15)

Help me accept that death is a part of life, Lord.

Spinning Sustainable Gold

When market researcher Jeremy Moon was handed a T-shirt by a farmer in New Zealand, his first impression was that "it didn't look too good, but it felt amazing."

Moon learned that the shirt was made from merino wool, giving it softness and resistance to odor. He was so inspired that he sought to "create a new category around natural-tech products." He researched New Zealand's sheep and wool.

When it was clear that the supply would not meet his demand, Moon essentially restructured the country's wool market. Buying for his company, Icebreaker, has helped increase stability for farmers.

More than that, each item can be traced back to its originating sheep, yielding a more sustainable, natural product than any other outdoor-clothing company can yet offer. All this innovation from one simple T-shirt!

Each of us needs to develop our vision, seeing beyond what's accepted today to what might become the norm tomorrow.

Prove me, O Lord, and try me; test my heart and mind. (Psalm 26:2)

Jesus, give us the wisdom and heart to find what inspires us, and bring that fire to others.

Living as the Hermit Within

In our fast-paced, stimulus-filled world, it's hard to imagine, let alone experience, silence and stillness. And yet, John Michael Talbot suggests that we can find both right on the spot we are standing.

In his book *The World Is My Cloister,* the Catholic monk states that we need not live in a monastery to know the peace of God and be a blessing to the world.

We can, instead, take a step back from the world in any moment, breathe, be calm and open mind and heart to "the still small voice within." Then we can see the world as God sees it—and be better able also to reflect God back to others.

Sometimes, pressing the "stop" button on the day's hustle and bustle can help us see and start down a better life direction.

If you would only keep silent, that would be your wisdom! (Job 13:5)

In the stillness, I listen for Your voice, Lord. Send me Your wisdom.

God and the Olympics

During the 2010 Winter Olympics in Vancouver, British Columbia, Monsignor Jerry Desmond strapped on skis and took the lift up a mountain. But he didn't ski.

Instead, from that point, he kept an eye on those headed down the mountain.

And when he wasn't looking out for the physical well-being of the athletes, the Iowa priest was helping care for their spiritual welfare. Monsignor Desmond was part of the team at a multi-faith center at Olympic Village.

"For those whose faith is a strong part of their life, that doesn't change in competition," he explained. "And those who face a specific challenge, seek counsel, encouragement and prayer."

Faith and daily living are truly connected, with our knowledge of a loving Creator who is a source of hope and strength.

Now faith is the assurance of things hoped for, the conviction of things not seen. (Hebrews 11:1)

Come to me, Redeemer, in our time of need. Hear our prayer.

Music Medicine

Country music stars are ready to record new songs—with words and music provided by young people.

Songwriter Jenny Plume was brought to Nashville's Monroe Carell Jr. Children's Hospital to start a music-therapy program. The children tell Plume a story, and she shapes the lyrics with them and comes up with a melody.

Country star Vince Gill recorded Chris Weber's composition, "That's Who I Am," telling the 17-year-old cystic fibrosis patient, "It's an honor to record your song."

"You'd be a fool not to say yes," Gill says of his participation in the program. "It's a chance to do something good in the world."

A smile, a kind word, a helping hand. Simple opportunities to make a difference for someone surround us every day.

Sing praises to the Lord, who dwells in Zion. (Psalm 9:11)

I praise You, Lord, through shouts of joy and whispered prayer.

Life Lessons from the Family Dog

Writer and *New York Times* editor Dana Jennings learned that he had an aggressive form of cancer. As he endured painful and tedious treatments, he found inspiration and wisdom from his elderly dog.

Bijou, a miniature poodle, is nearly unable to move around. She creaks as she walks, suffers from various ailments and spends most of her day on her doggie bed, snoozing.

Yet, "despite all her troubles and her advanced age, Bijou is still game," says Jennings. "She still barks at neighborhood dogs and groans to her feet for a walk."

Jennings adds that "Humans struggle with living in the present" while dogs "live in the moment by nature. Bijou eats when she's hungry and sleeps when she's tired."

Seek wisdom and inspiration in life's everyday experiences; in people and creatures; in Creation, itself.

To get wisdom is to love oneself.
(Proverbs 19:4)

Teach us to seek You and to find You, Holy Wisdom.

Learning How to Be a Father

"She told the doctor she didn't want nothing to do with the child," one young man recalled. "She just said, 'Forget you, and forget the baby.'"

But the new dad couldn't abandon their baby just because the mom wasn't ready to be a parent. Although he wasn't exactly ready either, he was willing to learn. Happily, there was help. The Fatherhood Program of the Visiting Nurse Service teaches young single fathers what it takes to be a parent.

"The program offers parenting workshops, conflict resolution training, counseling and day care," according to a *New York Daily News* story. "Participants learn how to change a diaper, handle a toddler's tantrum, and gain control over their own emotions so they can be the man who—in many cases—was never present in their own lives."

These young men need support from the community to fulfill their responsibilities. Encourage all new parents.

Fathers, do not provoke your children, or they may lose heart. (Colossians 3:21)

Heavenly Father, teach us to love our children the way You love us.

The Heart of the Matter

In San Antonio, Texas, priests from all corners of the globe participated in the International Priest Internship program at the Oblate School of Theology (OST).

OST's president, Father Ron Rolheiser, talked to them about ministry in America today, saying: "When the Gospel of John talks about God's house having many rooms, it's talking about the size of God's heart. Your task is to be minister to all of them, and it's an immense challenge."

His advice to the group was to emphasize the example of Jesus. Father Rolheiser told those gathered: "The challenge is to be universal as Jesus was. His love and compassion were for everybody. As priests, you have to have a heart for the liberals, a heart for conservatives and a heart for the people in the middle."

Each of us needs to open our hearts to every single one of God's children.

How very good and pleasant it is when kindred live together in unity. (Psalm 133:1)

It's easy to love what we like, Father, but hard to love what we do not. Show us how to love Your entire creation.

Hymn to the Treasure of Your Heart

An eighth-century Irish hymn offers thoughts worth pondering—and living:

Be Thou my vision, O Lord of my heart...

Be Thou my best thought in the day and night...

Be Thou my wisdom...

Be Thou my great Father, and I Thy true child...

Be Thou my breastplate, my sword for the fight;

Be Thou my whole armor, be Thou my true might...

Be Thou my soul's shelter, be Thou my strong tower...

Be Thou mine inheritance now and always...

Be Thou and Thou only the first in my heart.

If we try to live these words, we can truly sing with all our souls, "O Sovereign of heaven, my treasure Thou art."

The name of the Lord is a strong tower; the righteous run into it and are safe. (Proverbs 18:10)

Lord, You formed me and know me; remain with me.

Passing It On

When Ame Voilong was about 12 years old, he heard about Jesus from an Italian priest who had journeyed to Ame's homeland of Myanmar.

There, he taught the boy to pray, and even to compose hymns. Within a year, he was baptized by that missionary priest.

At the age of 20, Voilong married and moved with his wife to nearby Thailand. Almost 25 years later, the two are parents of five children, and now Voilong is like the missionary who first told him the Good News of Jesus.

He travels throughout his Thai village as well as back to Myanmar when he can, teaching and sharing his knowledge and experiences of the Lord. More than 50 people have been baptized through his instruction.

What brings us joy can also help others. Now there's some good news to shout about!

Therefore be imitators of God...and live in love, as Christ loved us. (Ephesians 5:1,2)

I pray to You, Eternal God, make me an enthusiastic witness of Your greatness and love.

A Tradition Born of Homage

Italian-Americans have a tradition of feeding people on the Feast of St. Joseph, a practice dating back to the Middle Ages in Italy.

When famine struck, people prayed to St. Joseph for rain and a bountiful harvest. When their prayers were answered, they showed their gratitude to the saint by preparing a feast for all. The custom, called a St. Joseph Table, continues.

A number of years ago in Chicago, Joseph Coco's young son suffered from rheumatic fever. Coco prayed to St. Joseph, promising that if his son were healed, he would feed the hungry at a St. Joseph Table. His prayers were answered, and Coco kept his word until his death 49 years later.

Now, his good friend and long-time associate, Peter Vito, carries the torch. There's only one rule for the dinner, says Vito, and that's that "No one is to be charged."

What traditions enliven your beliefs and spirituality?

So then...stand firm and hold fast to the traditions you were taught by us. (2 Thessalonians 2:15)

Remind us, Lamb of God, to respect all religions.

Undo the Spoiling

By one estimate, more than 90 percent of parents are worried their children are spoiled. According to Richard Bromfield, a Harvard Medical School psychologist, it's seldom too late to reverse the trend. He offers these tips for parents who want to take charge.

- Stand strong. Be firm in your authority, saying "no" without wavering or bargaining.

- Avoid idle threats. Threatening consequences you can't or won't implement is counterproductive. State your expectations realistically and clearly—and stick to them.

- Be a parent, not a pal. Children need and want discipline, even if just subconsciously. It promotes healthy growth into adulthood.

- Buy and do less. A child who grows up not getting everything he or she wants develops patience and an appreciation for life's gifts and blessings.

Prayer is the best partner for parents and all who help to nurture and love children as they grow.

Train children in the right way, and when old, they will not stray. (Proverbs 22:6)

Loving Father, we give thanks for Your love, given generously to us despite our weaknesses and failings.

Listen and Love

Have you ever "half listened" as someone tried to talk to you? Or felt yourself frustrated at not being heard by others?

Listening Is an Act of Love is the title of a book about Story Corps, a nonprofit organization whose mission it is to honor and celebrate people by interviewing them about their lives—and recording the conversation for posterity.

The first Story Booth was located in New York City's Grand Central Terminal several years ago. Today mobile recording booths travel around the country.

Men and women interview family members, friends, neighbors, teachers—and hear stories that may be humorous, instructive or heartbreaking. Recordings are archived and preserved at the Library of Congress.

Appreciate the value of the gift you give when you really listen to someone.

The wise listen to advice. (Proverbs 12:15)

Divine Master, help me learn to listen to others with the same attention I want You to hear me.

A Living Sign

As you enter Buffalo, New York, there's a sign announcing that it calls itself: "City of Good Neighbors." And folks here aren't just talking about next door; their neighbors are anyone around the globe.

Take Ann Marie Zon. She's turned her home into a center for outreach to the people of Nicaragua.

She and her father started helping in 1982, sending 22 boxes of school supplies that year to children in this Central American country. Now, as part of the Nicaragua Mission Project, she annually packs and sends more than 40,000 boxes of clothing, household items, canned goods and other such items, with donations and help from others in the area.

Frank Lewandowski makes similar shipments to Haiti. "What God has given us is to share," he says.

Next door, next town or next continent, there's a brother or sister in God's family in need of your love and prayers.

I give you a new commandment, that you love one another. Just as I have loved you, you should also love one another. (John 13:34)

Compassionate Father, help me to love as You do.

Picking Up Life's Pieces

For Sarah Rodriguez, it was turning into the worst day ever.

Her husband, Joel, had just finished his first week of chemotherapy. Being strong for him, she found herself worn out, exhausted physically and emotionally.

The couple's planned dinner with friends had to be cancelled because of complications from Joel's treatment. And then her favorite necklace broke into pieces.

It was the proverbial "last straw." Sarah ran into the bedroom, crying and begging God for a break.

When Sarah returned to the living room, her necklace was back together again, fished out of the trash and repaired by her husband.

"That's when God spoke to my heart," Sarah recalled, "telling me He'll fix what is broken, heal what is hurting."

God never gives up on us. Believing and trusting in that fact gives us hope and makes us whole.

I sought the Lord, and He answered me, and delivered me from all my fears. (Psalm 34:4)

Paraclete, I cry out to You for help. I believe in Your mercy.

It Takes Teamwork

Wise married couples know that to make their relationship work it's important to say *we, us and ours* more than *I, me and mine*.

A recent study determined that couples who try to resolve quarrels using lots of *I* phrases end up fighting bitterly. They also express more dissatisfaction with their marriage. But those who address their problems in the context of *we* do better. They seem happier and less stressed by disagreements.

Quoted in the *Edinburgh Scotsman*, researcher Robert Levenson said, "Individuality is a deeply ingrained value to society. But, at least in the realm of marriage, being part of a 'we' is well worth giving up a bit of 'me'."

It takes commitment and often hard work to overcome selfishness and resolve conflicts. Value individuality, but also nurture and strengthen the bond you have with your spouse.

Be subject to one another out of reverence for Christ. (Ephesians 5:21)

Guide my efforts to resolve differences with others, Holy Paraclete, especially those at home.

Sock Exchange

One snowy day in 1983, college freshman John Capuci saw a barefooted homeless man on the subway. Taking pity on the man's "red and raw feet," Capuci pulled off his own socks and gave them to him.

Now the pastor of St. Malachy's church in Burlington, Massachusetts, Father John Capuci oversees the monthly distribution of not only socks, but peanut butter and jelly sandwiches, bottled water and seasonal clothing to homeless people on the Boston Common. The generous efforts of St. Malachy's parish ensure that about 100 impoverished people receive help every month.

But the Burlington parishioners don't want their good deeds to end with them. "The big thing we're trying to do is get other parishes involved," said volunteer E.J. Landry.

Father Capuci ties his spur-of-the moment sock ministry to the biblical belief that works of charity should accompany a life of faith, for God is the first and greatest giver of all good things.

The one who sows bountifully will also reap bountifully. (2 Corinthians 9:6)

Oh Lord, help us to selflessly give to those in need, that our faith in Your infinite compassion may be strengthened.

Letting God into the Loneliness

Singer/songwriter Matt Maher had a big hit with his song "Your Grace is Enough," which was inspired by a time of intense loneliness in his life.

When Maher was a guest on our *Christopher Closeup* radio show/podcast, he shared his reflections on the challenge of loneliness.

He said, "I think a lot of people in this day and age feel disconnected from each other. They feel lonely at the end of the day. And the only way to (overcome) that is to get re-connected, primarily through God. Only God can meet all your expectations.

"We all have a desire to be loved deeply and be treasured. Sometimes we end up throwing that on people, and they can't match our expectations. We end up trying to love people out of our need rather than just loving people as a gift which is really how we're designed. We're designed to first be loved by God, and then to turn around and give that love away. When we do that, we're operating in the way that He made us."

Always remember that God created you and loves you.

My grace is sufficient for you, for power is made perfect in weakness. (2 Corinthians 12:9)

Lord, help me to appreciate Your love.

Doctor Delivers and Delivers

"It never gets boring to do a delivery. Every day a baby is born, it's a miraculous event," Dr. John Battaglino said about his long career.

The Wheeling, West Virginia, obstetrician and gynecologist retired after 47 years and 16,000 babies. Although mostly happy occasions, "there's nothing sadder than a stillbirth and to go through it with the parents," he said. "There's nothing you can do but cry along with the parents."

Dr. Battaglino has been working so long, some of the babies he delivered grew up to become doctors in the area. It's been an amazing career for a man who still ponders the mysteries of life.

"To think they start out as a microscopic egg and nine months later, there's a perfect human being," said Dr. Battaglino. "How a person could ever be an atheist, I don't know."

The world is full of God's wonders, but perhaps none is as beautiful as the birth of a baby.

Just as you do not know how the breath comes to the bones in the mother's womb, so you do not know the work of God, who makes everything. (Ecclesiastes 12:2)

Loving Father, remind me to appreciate the miracle of life.

A Pizza Box and Get-Well Wishes

When Monica Glick learned of her neighbor Bob's heart surgery, she wanted to help him fight the sense of isolation that illness often brings and help him keep a joy-filled focus.

On the back of a pizza box, she wrote the words, "We love you Bob!" She then took photographs with her phone's camera of people in their neighborhood holding the sign.

Monica e-mailed the images to Bob, one each day during his recuperation. In the end she had sent him 48 such photos.

Bob looked forward to seeing the "photo of the day," bolstered by the love of each smiling friend. He even printed all the photos, keeping them as a reminder of that source of hope in his life.

In love, we reach out to those in need—and draw from the love of others when we face our own dark days.

And now faith, hope, and love abide...and the greatest of these is love. (1 Corinthians 13:13)

Remind us of Your love, Merciful God, when we are alone and afraid.

About the Younger Generation

Unless you yourself were born between the late 1970s and the early 2000s, or have a child who was, it might be hard to recognize the unique characteristics of this age group sometimes called "Generation Y."

Yet research shows that these particular young people share some common traits. For one, public and community service is high on their list of priorities. One expert on the subject says, "These young adults want to be involved."

At the same time, because many of them were raised being told they could do anything, this generation shares a common trait of impatience for paying one's dues and might appear overconfident to older adults.

The fact is, people of every age have a great deal of good to offer. Get to know people of all backgrounds, beliefs and ages. You may be surprised at how much you learn!

Then He opened their minds to understand the scriptures. (Luke 24:45)

Don't let us judge by appearances, Lord of all.

Once Rejected, Now Independent

Twenty-eight-year-old Claudine Dhesi clearly remembers the attack on her village in the Democratic Republic of Congo by a different ethnic group. The gunshots whizzed by and the machete-wielding raiders flailed at everyone. One of them slashed her leg, which ultimately had to be amputated.

Then her husband abandoned her because of her disability and she was shuttled from one relative to another. All of them eventually turned her out, because "they thought I was useless," she says.

Today, thanks to Synergie Simama, a church-sponsored group, Dhesi is learning to make a living by training on sewing machines to be a skilled tailor. The group also helps restore the self-esteem so elusive to disabled victims of violence.

Says one priest affiliated with the effort, "We make friends with the vulnerable, walk in their shoes."

Find ways to reach out to those who are most vulnerable.

Blessed are the poor in spirit, for theirs is the Kingdom of heaven. (Matthew 5:3)

Protect the world's most vulnerable citizens, Merciful God.

There's Nun Better

NunBetter is a richly rewarding candy-making operation run by the Sisters of St. Francis.

At Easter time, their candy store offers such treats as "malted balls, jelly beans, chocolate cups with peanut butter and dark chocolate with nuts," writes Jennika Baines in *The Catholic Sun* of Syracuse, New York.

NunBetter "got started because a lot of the religious communities were looking for something to bring in more income," said Sister Jane Bourne, OSF.

The endeavor helps the retired nuns socially and financially. As the nuns work to fill chocolate molds, price bags of candy and wrap gift boxes, they also chat about politics, the weather, sports and other local events. "It's very relaxing and we have a great deal of fun while we're working," said one.

Sometimes, solutions to one problem can solve others as well, if we just stay open to new ideas.

God will fully satisfy every need of yours according to His riches in glory in Christ Jesus (Philippians 4:19)

Redeemer, encourage me to open my mind to new possibilities.

From a Single Project, a Spiritual Journey

In 2008, Mary Ann Ruppert's parish priest asked her to help repaint a few of the church's Stations of the Cross—the carved, wooden images that depict the final hours of Christ's Passion. The images had become worn and in need of careful restoration through detailed repainting.

"I jumped at the chance," says the 72-year-old Ruppert, who always enjoyed art but had not found the time or opportunity to paint seriously.

What Ruppert didn't expect was the time-consuming nature of the task. "Sometimes I spend hours doing a face because I want to get the right expression," she says.

But the arduous process led Ruppert to a deeper meaning of work, talent and mission. "We are called to use the gifts and talents we have been given in God's Kingdom," she says.

How can you use your unique gifts for the glory of God?

Each of us was given grace according to the measure of Christ's gift...to equip the saints for the work of...building up the body of Christ. (Ephesians 4:7-12)

Divine Creator, remind us to be generous with our talents.

A Dream Delivered

Twelve-year-old Joel Hasken always dreamed of being a letter carrier. While other children were playing video games, he played with a toy mailbox and followed his mailman, Bruce Beu, on his route in Elgin, Illinois.

Although Joel's autism made it difficult to communicate, he was extremely social. Even when he developed a brain tumor and was hospitalized, Joel insisted on greeting each new acquaintance. Joel's tumor only gave him months to live, so his mother set about ensuring her son's dream of being a letter carrier.

With the help of church parishioner and mailman John Serrato, Joel Hasken was named an honorary member of the Elgin Post Office. Since his paralysis rendered him unable to deliver mail, the Post Office sent a parade of postal vehicles past the Haskens' home in recognition of the honor. Joel died later that same evening.

"I believe it was God's timing," said Serrato, "that the Post Office got to present this to him while he was still alive."

God's timing—and a lot of compassionate hearts.

Abide in My love. (John 15:10)

Dear Lord, give me the courage and strength to follow my dreams.

Medical Miracle

The first thing three-year-old Chase's parents want people to know is that he's happy. His mom, Heather, says, "His life is to make people smile. He's got so much love around him."

Chase, who is legally blind, was born prematurely without a cerebellum. The doctors are baffled by his good condition. One said, "That's impossible. He has the MRI of a vegetable."

But Chase is not a vegetable. Even though he is also missing the part of his brain which controls basic functions, Chase has managed to sit up on his own, can crawl, and is learning to walk.

His mom says, "Don't believe everything the doctors say. Don't get me wrong. I love doctors. But they can be wrong. Chase is extremely healthy. And he's extremely smart—his motor skills just haven't caught up yet. People can view this as a tragic story. But that depends on how you look at life. You can be angry or you can appreciate what you've been given. Chase was meant to be with us."

Appreciate what you've been given.

I command you: be firm and steadfast! Do not fear nor be dismayed, for the Lord, your God, is with you wherever you go. (Joshua 9:9)

Thank You for my life, Lord; all things are possible in You!

Court Upholds Crucifixes

In 2009, a lower chamber of the European court ruled that crucifixes in classrooms violated the religious-freedom clauses of the European Convention of Human Rights.

The lawsuit, initiated by a mother who claimed the crucifix violated her children's freedom of conscience, was opposed by many, including the Catholic Church, the Orthodox Church, and the Italian government, which said they are a sign of Christianity's contributions to European civilization and culture.

Two years later, the Grand Chamber of the European court ruled that hanging crucifixes in Italian classrooms does not violate the consciences of non-Catholic families. Cardinal Giano Ravasi, president of the Pontifical Council for Culture, said, "Even if someone does not want to recognize it, it is an objective fact that the Christian presence is absolutely relevant and decisive."

Defense of religion needs to take place in the legal sphere as well as in our families and communities.

New gods were their choice; then the war was at their gates...the people of the Lord came down for me as warriors. (Judges 5:8,13)

Lord, give us strength to defend You!

This Show Must—and Does—Go On

It's a visual spectacle and a musical feast. Yet its history is equally inspiring to audiences lucky enough to see a performance of the Oberammergau, Germany, Passion Play.

The show has unique beginnings. In 1633, the townspeople of this tiny village panicked when a deadly plague swept through, killing 80 townsfolk—a sizable portion of the town in those days.

The villagers pledged to perform a play depicting the suffering, death and resurrection of Jesus Christ every 10 years if they were spared further pestilence and destruction. The disease halted. The following year, the first presentation of the town's Passion Play took place. Since then, few obstacles have prevented this special show from going on.

Spectators say the event is breathtaking, especially the score composed in the early 1800s, as well as the costumes and scenery.

Traditions come in many forms. Respect and honor those that are part of your religious heritage.

I commend you because you remember me in everything and maintain the traditions just as I handed them on to you. (1 Corinthians 11:2)

Help me discern Your wisdom, Yahweh.

Rediscovering Simplicity in Prayer

Writing in *The Catholic Weekly*, Central Michigan University freshman Lissi Schick explained that maintaining her prayer life, particularly during Lent, proved to be difficult.

In the midst of all her academic and familial obligations, Schick struggled to carve out a small space of time for the Lord. Even more discouraging was the fact that she didn't feel better after praying.

Schick asked herself countless times: "Why do I feel as though I am trying to force a response out of God? What am I doing wrong?"

She found the answer to these questions in the 10th Station of the Cross, during which Jesus was stripped of all of his earthly possessions, facing God in utter poverty. In this same meek manner, Schick concluded, she should at all times approach the Lord in prayer. Quite literally, Schick believed that her prayers had to be stripped back down to their humble basics.

Praying can truly be as simple as being fully and completely present with God. Remember, the Lord hears everyone's prayers, big or small, spoken or unspoken.

Persevere in prayer. (Romans 12:12)

Lord, help us to be as present in our prayers as we are fervent.

Teacher of Love

When Mother Teresa was working at a mission in Venezuela, a local family dropped a lamb off as a gift for the nuns.

Mother Teresa went to visit the family to thank them for their generosity. When she arrived, she saw that they were caring for a crippled child. She asked the mother, "What is the child's name?"

The mother responded, "We call him 'Teacher of Love' because he keeps teaching us how to love. Everything we do for him is our love for God in action."

Though caring for someone who is disabled or infirm can be challenging, that mother's statement offers an important perspective.

Look at those who can't care for themselves, not as a burden, but as people who can teach us about love, patience, compassion, mercy, and humility. You'll be sharing God's love in one of the most meaningful ways possible—and growing in divine virtues yourself.

God is love, and those who abide in love abide in God, and God abides in them. (1 John 4:16)

Lord, help us appreciate the inherent dignity of all Your children.

From Darkness into the Light

After 69 days underground, all 33 of the trapped Chilean miners emerged. Months later, they took a pilgrimage to the Holy Land for a week, visiting Jewish and Christian holy sites.

One miner named Jose expressed the privilege he felt to be in Jerusalem.

"We are happy to be close to the place of God and to be able to thank the thousands who prayed for our return. This visit is also a chance for us to strengthen our faith in Jesus," he said.

Another miner, Richard, spent most of his time underground praying that he would see his pregnant wife again. Six days after he was rescued, his son was born. "I lost count of the number of Ave Marias and Our Fathers I said while I was trapped," Richard said. "Prayer gave me the strength not to get depressed."

His wife, Dana, said, "When he was in the mine I felt the Holy Spirit, and my faith was strong. I want to thank God, and here is the best place to do that."

We were indeed buried with Him through baptism into death, so that, just as Christ was raised from the dead by the glory of the Father, we too might live in newness of life. (Romans 6:4)

Risen Lord, we are grateful for Your salvation.

Safe Landing

On one busy Easter Sunday, Lisa Grimm, an air traffic controller in Miami, heard these words: "My pilot's deceased. I need help."

The voice belonged to Doug White, a passenger on the plane, along with his wife and two daughters. Their pilot had become ill and died at 10,000 feet. White, a private pilot himself, had never flown an aircraft as big and powerful as the one he and his family were now on.

Grimm and five other air traffic controllers helped White hand-fly the plane to safety. The six were honored for their efforts.

In our own lives, we should never hesitate to ask for someone's help—and we should always be ready to guide a soul to safety.

Commit your way to the Lord; trust in Him, and He will act. (Psalm 37:5)

With Your help, Father, all things are possible.

Choosing the Right Volunteer Opportunity

Gayle Elleven of Fort Worth, Texas, wanted to make an impact through volunteering. Then a friend told her that educational charities are effective, because they help break the cycle of poverty.

She took the advice to heart, and went online to find the right place to devote her volunteer hours. She tried volunteermatch.org, a site which enables seekers to find charitable organizations based on type and location.

Today, Elleven devotes three hours a week to tutor adults who read on a second- to sixth-grade level. The impact of her efforts is demonstrated through her students. "One woman I tutored is now taking college courses, working toward a degree," Elleven says.

Find a cause or organization in sympathy with your own interests and passion, and the effect you have will be life-changing!

Does not a word surpass a good gift? Both are to be found in a gracious person. (Sirach 18:17)

Broaden my capacity for generosity, Jesus, my Lord and Brother.

Easy Ways to Live Longer

Have you heard about the "Power 9?"

Dan Buettner, researcher and writer about the subject of longevity, has identified nine health-producing behaviors through his studies of communities with longer-than-average life spans. Some of these factors are predictable, others a bit more surprising:

- Keep moving. Walk, garden, etc. to stay active.
- Find a purpose and pursue it with passion.
- Slow down. Take more vacations, if possible.
- Stop eating when you're nearly full.
- Dine on plants. Choose vegetables over processed foods.
- Drink red wine consistently but in moderation.
- Join a group. Maintain a solid social network.
- Feed your soul through spiritual activities.
- Make family a high priority.

Whatever your age, live your life with joy!

Old age is not honored for length of time, or measured by number of years; but understanding is gray hair for anyone, and a blameless life is ripe old age. (Wisdom of Solomon 4:8-9)

Lord Jesus, help us make healthful choices.

Not Taking "No" for an Answer

The ongoing healthcare debate in America has focused largely on the uninsured. But what about those who have health insurance but face repeated claim rejections from insurers?

Kevin Lembo, a patient advocate who helps Connecticut families negotiate with insurers, says, "Don't accept the insurance company's word as final. It is not, nor should it be."

Experts suggest the following if your claim is denied:

Keep records, especially documentation that your doctor determined that the treatment prescribed was needed.

Build your case before appealing. Create an organized, accessible and easy-to-follow file tracking your claim.

Get the reason for the claim denial in writing.

Seek the advice of a local non-profit group that assists patients dealing with insurers.

Stay polite and persistent in seeking any goal.

You shall not abuse any widow or orphan...If you do abuse them, when they cry out to Me, I will surely hear their cry. (Exodus 22:22-23)

Embolden us in our pursuit of justice, Divine Master.

Patient Music

Singer-songwriter Carla Ulbrich toured up and down the East Coast of the United States.

Then she had a stroke—two, in fact, within a three-day period, affecting her left foot and hand.

Ulbrich was off the touring circuit for the remainder of that year, trying to get her health under control—and finding a productive, but quirky path back to music. She started writing off-beat songs about medical encounters, from the trying side effects of medications to the sometimes dignity-robbing diagnostic tests.

Known as "The Singing Patient," Ulbrich explains, "I want caregivers to know that they really do make a difference and I want to make patients laugh about something they usually cry about."

Life may, at times, be packed with unpleasant experiences. How good to be able to seek and find joy peeping out from beneath the pain!

The unfolding of Your words gives light. (Psalm 119:130)

In every smile, there is a glimpse of Your joy, Father.

The "Average" Dad?

The definition of an average dad has changed over time—at least on TV. In the 1950s, Dad worked a 9-to-5 job in a suit and arrived home in the evening, ready to offer quips or advice as needed.

Today, television shows a decidedly different image. In some shows, fathers are bumbling buffoons outsmarted by their own children. In others, the father figure is clueless—relying on his wife or grown children to fill him in on reality. In some cases, Dad is simply absent.

Real fatherhood is demanding, exhausting and often thankless. So where do the negative stereotypes come from?

According to the Media Awareness Network, an organization that examines media bias, such portrayals hook wide audiences with "boiled-down" images of certain segments of society. In short, stereotyping sells.

Develop greater mindfulness of media biases and stereotyping. Oppose such practices through thoughtful and respectful letters and e-mails.

Exhort one another...that none of you may be hardened by the deceitfulness of sin. (Hebrews 3:13)

Help us remember that our precious right to free speech requires diligence and responsibility, Blessed Trinity.

Soldier Forgives Suicide Bomber

On April 6, 2005, Captain Scotty Smiley was on patrol with his platoon in Iraq. A suicide bomber exploded a car bomb that sent shrapnel and debris into Captain Smiley's eyes and brain, permanently destroying his vision.

The young officer was crushed by the news he would never see again. Despite coming from a religious family, he admits, "I definitely questioned God." Also, hatred for the bomber led Captain Smiley into months of depression.

On our *Christopher Closeup* radio show/podcast, he explained that he was moved toward forgiveness by contemplating the scriptural instruction to love your brother as yourself. "[When] I made that effort to forgive him," Captain Smiley said, "that's when I was able to move out of depression and begin to start taking a positive step forward."

Captain Smiley went on to become the Army's first blind active-duty officer, commander of the Warrior Transition Unit for wounded soldiers, and winner of the 2011 Christopher Leadership Award.

Let go of any anger that prevents you from living fully.

Blessed are the merciful. (Matthew 5:7)

Lord, take away the burden of resentment I carry.

When Words and Actions Don't Match

Michael Josephson, a speaker and radio commentator, tells the story of Matt, an eighth-grade teacher who tried to bend the rules.

Matt was in a hurry as he shopped for last-minute items for a gathering at his home. His basket held 14 items, but he went to the "10 Items or Less" checkout line.

When Matt noticed one of his students, Phil, approaching him, he saw that he'd set a bad example. Sure enough, the student said, "You have too many items, and that's cheating."

Matt realized that the disconnect between his words and actions could seriously undermine his message to his students about the importance of ethics, not to mention his own credibility.

Josephson concludes, "If what you're thinking of doing isn't consistent with the image you want to convey, don't do it."

That's good advice for each of us—whether anyone else is watching or not.

The righteous walk in integrity — happy are the children who follow them! (Proverbs 20:7)

Keep me honest, Holy Spirit.

Taking the Mugger to Dinner

Every night after work, Julio Diaz would get off the New York City subway one stop before his home, just so he could eat at his favorite diner.

One night as Diaz got off the train, a teenage boy approached, holding a knife and demanding Diaz's wallet. Diaz surrendered the wallet, then called after the young man as he walked away.

Diaz offered his coat on the cold evening, and then invited the teen to dinner. "I just felt he really needed help," Diaz recalled later.

The two went to the diner, and when the check came, Diaz said, "I guess you're paying since you have my money. But if you give me my wallet back, I'll gladly treat you." The youth surrendered the wallet—and the knife too, when asked for it. Diaz gave him $20.

Simple acts of kindness can transform a heart's direction for the better.

The mind of the wise makes their speech judicious, and adds persuasiveness to their lips. (Proverbs 16:23)

Help me, Father, to meet challenging times with Your compassion and love.

Miracle Cure?

Is there such a thing as a magic health food? Can any single item help prevent inflammation, reduce diabetes symptoms, protect against some cancers?

Well, onions aren't magical, but they are pretty amazing, with many cultures considering them to be almost "cure-alls," according to *Prevention* magazine.

New studies confirm the value of many traditional uses of onions. Olympians in ancient Greece were on to something when they ate onions and drank their juice.

Modern nutritionists report that the quercetin extract from onions increases endurance. It's a flavonoid that also protects against stomach ulcers as well as colon, esophageal and breast cancers. Meanwhile, the sulfur compounds in onions reduce diabetes symptoms and protect against cardiovascular disease.

Many scientists advise eating onions regularly along with other fruits and vegetables.

Not magic, but good advice.

You cause the grass to grow for the cattle, and plants for people to use, to bring forth food from the earth. (Psalm 104:14)

Generous Father, thank You for Your many gifts, including those that contribute to health and healing.

Riding a Positive Wave

Seeing children in a seaside community learn to surf is not unusual. But it becomes a moment to treasure when those young people have disabilities ranging from near-blindness to autism.

"The feeling of riding a wave is like nothing else," says professional surfer Cliff Skudin, who founded Surf for All. His is one of many programs giving special-needs children the chance to experience that feeling.

He recalls working with one autistic child who had never spoken. After riding the wave with Skudin, the child shouted, "More, more, I want more."

"To see that was awesome," Skudin says.

Helping someone overcome difficulties or achieve success is "awesome" as well.

Since there will never cease to be some in need on the earth, I therefore command you, "Open your hand to the poor and needy." (Deuteronomy 15:11)

This day, bless my work, Lord.

A Mix of Mother Teresa and Rambo

Dr. Hawa Abdi has been a doctor in her native Somalia for three decades. Working first for government hospitals, she eventually opened a one-room clinic.

That facility has grown into a 400-bed hospital, where Dr. Abdi and her staff—including her two daughters who are doctors—treat everything from malaria to malnutrition, life-threatening in her war-torn homeland.

When she and her hospital were attacked by militants, she refused to leave. "If I die, I will die with my people and my dignity," she told them. They left after several days, and later even apologized for the attack.

In honoring her efforts, one magazine described her as "equal parts Mother Teresa and Rambo." In writing about her, another author observed: "Dr. Hawa and her daughters have built a city of healing within the war's brutal chaos."

Each of us is also called to work for healing and peace in our daily reality.

Because you have made the Lord your refuge, the Most High your dwelling place, no evil shall befall you, no scourge come near your tent. (Psalm 91:9)

Send Your Spirit, Lord, to calm my fears and give me courage.

A Lost Art, to Be Restored

When Monsignor John T. Doherty died in January, 2010, at age 89, *Catholic New York* honored his memory by publishing a column he wrote in 1984 in which he lamented the lost art of "looking out the window."

In a time before high rises, he wrote, watching the world go by was a shared experience, a way of seeing and connecting to one's community. It was a time where entertainment was found in the observation of everyday life.

"But then came the man who invented the elevator. And the tall apartments, the sky-high projects and the high-rise living followed. The streets became anonymous. But we found another way. We began to watch life on a screen that was placed just inside the window that was closed and curtained."

Even if we no longer watch from our windows, we can still care for our community by extending ourselves to our neighbors day by day.

The compassion of human beings is for their neighbors, but the compassion of the Lord is for every living thing. (Sirach 18:13)

Light of Love, let us not forget our ties of fellowship to each other and Your whole creation.

Scouting Possibilities

Teen Richard Herbers wasn't playing around as he tried to earn Scouting's highest rank, Eagle Scout—although his project did involve revamping a local children's playground.

Herbers' four brothers, father, seven uncles and seven cousins were all Boy Scouts. His family, along with friends, pitched in on the park project. In the end, nearly 30 volunteers put in more than 100 hours to complete the structure.

"I think because of his leadership, his friends—not just scouts, but others—wanted to come and help him," explained his mother, Norma.

And his service now and in the future is important to Herbers. "I want to make sure that I do everything for the right judgment, not just because it will be fun or because of peer pressure," he explained.

All we do for others starts with love of neighbor—rooted in, of course, our great love for God!

Jesus answered..."You shall love your neighbor as yourself." (Mark 12:29-31)

Lord, in all I do, may I reflect Your boundless love.

A National Hero

For Hung Ba Le—the first ever Vietnamese-American Navy captain—the Vietnam War was more than just a conflict between North and South; it was a life-altering journey.

Five-year-old Le fled war-torn Vietnam in a boat with his family. They were rescued by a U.S. Navy ship and able to settle in Virginia.

Le's father, a Navy captain in his native South Vietnam, worked his way up to supermarket manager to support his family. His son, who graduated from the United States Naval Academy in 1992, was eventually elevated to the position of commander and currently directs the helm of the USS Lassen.

In Vietnam, Le is a "celebrity." In the United States, he is highly commended for his naval achievements. His greatest inspiration, however, remains his father. Le says, "I looked to my dad as a Navy commander for his country and I wanted to follow in his footsteps. He's my hero."

Give thanks for the heroes in your life, and be sure to let them know how much their example of persevering through hardship means to you.

Bear fruit with patient endurance. (Luke 8:15)

Lord, let the example of the inspiring people in our lives give us the courage and strength to achieve our dreams.

From Slavery to Possible Sainthood

On April 24, 1886, at St. John Lateran Basilica in Rome, Augustine Tolton became the first known black U.S. priest.

Just 32 years before, he had been born into slavery in Brush Creek, Missouri, with little hope for any life but one of toil and misery.

His rise from bondage to ministry is an extraordinary tale, and now the Archdiocese of Chicago, where Father Tolton tirelessly served black Catholics from 1889 until his death in 1897, is seeking his canonization.

Father Tolton's successful struggle out of chains and into leadership in the spiritual life of his community shows that we can not only help ourselves but those around us. By trusting in God we can transcend circumstances and defy the odds, achieving far more than we ever thought possible.

Don't let hardships weaken your resolve or extinguish your dreams. Have faith that God will lead you to a better future.

Cast your burden on the Lord, and He will sustain you. (Psalm 55:22)

Let me remember that You are always with me, Spirit of Compassion, even in times of difficulty.

Not a "Baaaaaad" Second-Career Option

Tough economic times seem to elicit reflection on one's path in life, specifically concerning career. As a result, it's not unusual for people to embark on a second (or even third) career when the economy takes a downturn. If you're in the same boat, here's an idea for a new career: raising goats.

It's true—raising goats is a veritable career that one can undertake. If you're interested, you may want to apply early, though; the U.S. has only one school that trains aspiring goatherds.

Stony Knolls Farm in Maine boasts a 28-acre picturesque "campus" that is called home by 30 goats of various breeds. Before you scoff, you should know that a recent class at the Farm was at full capacity, having attracted over 110 students from 22 states, including doctors, lawyers and former FBI agents.

How do you respond to life's challenges? Think outside the box. And remember: With God, anything is possible.

You need endurance, so that when you have done the will of God, you may receive what was promised. (Hebrews 10:35-36)

Grant me the wisdom and courage to turn failure into opportunity, Jesus.

Holy Land Patrol

In the spirit of interfaith understanding, a group of New York City police officers journeyed to the Holy Land.

"For me, this was all about unity and togetherness," said Detective Lawrence Wein, head of the New York City Police Department's Jewish organization, the Shomrim Society.

"It's one thing to be respectful of something," explained Sergeant Brian Reilly of the Catholic Holy Name Society. "It's another thing to understand it."

Visiting Christian, Muslim and Jewish holy sites in the Holy Land and Egypt, all were inspired to learn more about the faith traditions of others.

"This will help make us better people and better police officers," said Detective Ahmed Nasser of the Muslim Officers Society. "And with God's help, we'll continue to do so."

Each of us can find joy and peace knowing we're all part of God's family.

May the Lord grant you discretion and understanding. (1 Chronicles 22:12)

Gather us in, Father, to live in Your peace and Your love.

Men, Women and Friendship

Friendship is important to all of us, although men and women may express their feelings differently.

Speaking of time spent with his buddies, one man tells columnist and author Jeffrey Zaslow, "It's a judgment-free, action-packed, adventure-based weekend. We go hiking, whitewater rafting, rock climbing, fly-fishing." Zaslow himself regularly plays poker with his friends but the men rarely discuss their personal lives.

"I envy women's easy intimacy. I also know it wouldn't work for me and my friends," writes Zaslow. He cites studies at the University of Maryland School of Social Work showing that male and female friendships tend to be different, with women being more physically and emotionally expressive.

Still, men and women alike can derive great support from their friendships. They may take different forms, but they're valuable nevertheless.

Thus the Lord used to speak to Moses face to face, as one speaks to a friend. (Exodus 33:11)

My Lord, my Friend, teach me to treasure our relationship above all others.

Caring in the Wake of Disaster

Tornadoes, tsunamis, explosions, earthquakes. At times there seems no end to disasters or to the 24/7 news coverage about them.

Immediate crises eventually end and reporters leave the scene. But what remains, often for a long time, are traumatized victims and caregivers. In the wake of the devastating earthquake in Haiti are the countless numbers left homeless.

Some fortunate Haitians got to the United States where loved ones opened their arms and their doors. Still, even though generous families assist earthquake survivors, they must all deal with the stress of living doubled up.

Their guests lack everything from adequate clothing to job prospects. Many are still suffering emotional distress. And these are the lucky few. Those back home have even less.

After the next newsworthy disaster, know that the struggles go on after the cameras go off. But so does the caring.

We ought to support such people, so that we may become co-workers with the truth. (3 John 1:8)

Remind us to pray for and support people who are in trouble even when others have forgotten them, Holy Spirit.

Living to Make a Difference

For Kiran Yocum, life's all about making a difference in one person's life. "If you can do that, you did it all," she says.

Born in India, she came to the United States as an adult in 1995. Three years later, she started Seniors Helping Seniors, a non-profit organization which has helped thousands of elderly people live independently in their own homes. Within a decade, she franchised the concept nationwide.

"I give credit to God for this growth," Yocum explains. "It is God who wants to see us help so many with the power of love."

The difference we make for someone this day could be as simple as a warm smile or a listening heart. Be that source of support for anyone in need.

You shall rise before the aged, and defer to the old; and you shall fear your God: I am the Lord. (Leviticus 19:32)

Through the power of Your love, Jesus, help me to act in accordance with Your will.

Stopping Stress — As Easy As ABC

According to the Midwest Center, a provider of help for people suffering from anxiety and depression, removing stress from your life is as easy as ABC.

- **A**ttitude: A positive attitude can help you convert bad stress to good stress. For example, instead of being stressed out about a particular task or situation, instead feel excited about the potential for new experiences. And try to surround yourself with similar positive thinkers!

- **B**reathe: Calm down, by slowing down, starting with your breathing.

- **C**hoice: Choose to control what you can—and that's rarely the words and actions of others. Make choices to do things to the best of your ability and with an open heart, at home or on the job.

And a key stress reliever is, of course, a prayer to the Source of all life and hope, the Lord. "Come and rest in Me." That's an invitation not to be forgotten!

Are not five sparrows sold for two pennies? Yet not one of them is forgotten in God's sight... You are of more value than many sparrows. (Luke 12:6-7)

Bless me with Your peace, Lord.

Set Your Feet Toward Hope

Cheers erupted from the crowd as 95-year-old Ida Keeling finished the 60-meter race in 29.28 seconds, setting a new world record for runners age 95 and up.

Years ago, Ida didn't feel much like walking, let alone running. Her husband had died of a heart attack at 42. About 20 years later, both her sons were murdered. It was her daughter Shelly, a lawyer who also coached track and field, who suggested her mother try a 5K race in Brooklyn.

Ida, who had suffered from high blood pressure following her tragic life events, immediately saw her health improve after she began running. When she completed that first race, she told the *Riverdale Press* in New York City that she "felt great" and "didn't want to stop."

That was nearly three years ago and, as the recent race record shows, Ida is still running.

Do you feel that you need something to "recharge" your life? Find your passion and stick with it—you'll be glad you did!

I have finished the race, I have kept the faith. (2 Timothy 4:7)

Lord, give me the strength to endure life's dark times and stay focused on a winning future.

Real Men and Rosaries

"I thought the rosary was for old ladies and funerals," said David Calvillo of McAllen, Texas, who didn't respond to his mother's urging that he pray the rosary in his youth. Years later it would be different.

He agreed to attend a retreat, although he was hesitant because he didn't know what to expect. But it changed his life.

"As we were praying the rosary at the retreat," said Calvillo, "I saw something that I had never seen before. I felt this incredible connection."

After more prayer, study and fellowship with other men of faith, Calvillo formed an apostolate called Real Men Pray the Rosary. He also created its logo with a man's tough-looking hand clutching a rosary. The movement has proved popular. Members also actually create and distribute rosaries.

Open yourself to prayer in its various forms to enliven your spiritual growth.

Call to Me and I will answer you, and will tell you great and hidden things that you have not known. (Jeremiah 33:3)

Teach me to pray, Jesus, Lord, Brother and Friend.

Kindness to Start the Morning

Maggie had felt sad for days.

In a week's time, she had attended the wakes of the mothers of a co-worker and a good friend. Then came the particularly sorrowful wake of another friend's young adult son, just in his early 20s.

Getting up late one morning, she raced to make the train to work. She realized she'd forgotten her favorite bracelet, but didn't have time to return for it.

At the station, she spotted a neighbor and her six-year-old daughter. The child greeted Maggie with a big smile and hug. Then the child took off the shiny bangle she was wearing and handed it to Maggie saying, "This is just what you need."

"Yes it is," Maggie agreed, brightened by the loving act.

In every moment, even the smallest of gestures can bring light to someone's life.

You must make every effort to support your faith with goodness. (2 Peter 1:5)

Through my darkness, Lord, shine Your loving light.

A Spiritual Lift

Unable to see, talk or move his limbs because of cerebral palsy, eight-year-old Sammy Parker must be carried up the stairs to bed every night. Previously, it was Sammy's father who performed this task. After his recent surgery, however, Rudy Favard, a senior at Malden Catholic High School, was happy to step in.

The Massachusetts school's nurse first alerted Rudy to the opportunity and he immediately volunteered his services. Sammy quickly grew to adore his surrogate brother figure.

Although Rudy physically carries Sammy, it is Sammy who spiritually lifts him. Rudy said later, "He's done more for me than I've done for him…I've never been one to complain a lot, but just seeing Sam reaffirms everything."

Rudy will be going to college, so the Parkers hope to move to a house with no stairs. None of them, however, will ever forget this life-changing human experience of giving and receiving far more than they ever expected in return.

Consider giving someone a spiritual lift today. Your life will be richer for your efforts.

Those who wait for the Lord shall renew their strength, they shall mount up with wings like eagles. (Isaiah 40:31)

Lord, help me to ease someone's burdens.

Kids Only for a Day

In Japan, every May 5 is *Kodomo no Hi*— "Children's Day."

Families fly *koinobori* banners in the shape of a carp—one for each child in the household. In Japanese folklore, the carp is a symbol of determination and vigor, as that particular fish overcomes all obstacles to swim upstream. *Samurai* warrior figures are also displayed to inspire strength and bravery.

Children indulge in sweet rice cakes, and other treats. They also take center stage in traditional Japanese plays. Thousands of young people compete in a Kids' Olympics at the National Stadium in Tokyo, and there are many other such events throughout the country.

On this special children's day, the young are asked also to say "thanks" to their parents and all who care for them.

Every day, every person should be celebrated and loved, as each offers an abundance of gratitude.

All your children shall be taught by the Lord, and great shall be the prosperity of your children. (Isaiah 54:13)

How blessed I am to call You "Father!" How blessed to be one in the family of God!

A Real-Life Samaritan

For LeMoyne College junior Andrew Lunetta, being a Good Samaritan isn't just a biblical concept—it's a real-life aspiration.

Lunetta established a program at his school in which students make sandwiches that are delivered to the aptly named Samaritan Center. His charity work extends far beyond his Syracuse community, however.

Lunetta taught English to people in Central Mexico during 2010. Then he traveled to the town of Nogales, Mexico, to work with the Kino Board Initiative, an organization that provides aid to immigrants who have been deported from the U.S. This experience, he said, taught him about "the importance of the human connection, how important it is to let one express oneself."

"I'm definitely excited for the future," Lunetta admits. "I've met so many good people because of this path I've chosen."

Invite God into your chosen path of life and you'll never be steered wrong.

Trust in the Lord...In all your ways acknowledge Him, and He will make straight your paths. (Proverbs 3:5-6)

Lord, grant me the courage to walk on my chosen path knowing that You are beside me, guiding my steps.

Making the Crooked Straight

Motivated to help others by the Orthodox Jewish belief that he who saves one life saves an entire world, Dr. Rick Hodes first flew to Ethiopia in 1984 as a relief worker during the famine.

Witnessing the great need for doctors, he chose to live in Ethiopia where he now works at one of Mother Teresa's missions, treating many Christian and Muslim children suffering from potentially fatal spinal deformities.

Dr. Hodes discovered that it would be easier to care for some of the kids if they lived with him, so he's also acted as a foster parent to 17 children, providing them with a loving home, an education, and vital medical care.

The Christophers were pleased to honor a documentary about Dr. Hodes called *Making the Crooked Straight* with a Christopher Award in 2011, because it shone a light on this selfless man whose life is a model of faith, hope, and charity.

May the same words be used to describe all our lives.

I have aroused Cyrus in righteousness, and I will make all his paths straight; he shall build my city and set my exiles free. (Isaiah 45:13)

May our lives testify to the fact that everyone is created in Your image and likeness, Lord.

Always In There Swinging

At the age of 7, Michelle McGann was swinging a golf club and hitting a good drive.

Six years later, she was diagnosed with type 1 diabetes. "I remember asking if I could still play golf," recalls McGann, who, at age 23, would lead the U.S. Women's Open after only four hours of play.

Although diabetes cost her that competition—out-of-control blood sugar caused her to miss six or seven shots—eventually she got her condition under control. Today, she and her husband have started a foundation to help young people with diabetes.

"My biggest goal is to let them know that they can control diabetes, and not let it control them," McGann said.

In life, we confront challenges and face fears. With courage and God's grace, we can triumph and even make life better for others.

O Lord my God, I cried to You for help, and You have healed me. (Psalm 30:2-3)

Bless us with Your hope, Loving Master. Lift us from despair.

Cleveland Goes Green

Cleveland, Ohio, a once-booming industrial city, wracked in recent years by economic decline and a spate of foreclosures, has reinvented itself as a leader in environmental renewal. Today it's a model for other cities trying to give decaying neighborhoods a new lease on life.

In 2008, Cleveland officials started a program that transforms condemned properties into public gardens. Over 225 of these green patches now dot the city, along with two dozen farmers' markets, and a popular community agriculture movement.

The resilience and creativity shown by this city in the face of hardship teaches a valuable lesson. When confronted with serious difficulties, don't give up.

You *can* turn hard times into a fresh start. Meet challenges with determination and some outside-the-box thinking. It's difficult, but well worth the effort.

Be steadfast and do not be impetuous in time of calamity. Cling to Him. (Sirach 2:2)

Spirit of Counsel, give me the courage and creativity to turn my problems into chances for positive change.

Argue Responsibly

Everyone knows that disagreements are part of every relationship. But did you know that there's a right way to argue, and that doing so can ultimately make your relationships stronger?

Here are some tips from the *Wall Street Journal* for turning angry arguments into something more productive:

- Talk about problems. Ignoring issues won't make them go away.

- Cool off. Choose a time to return to the discussion after emotions have subsided.

- Be flexible. Changing your position isn't "losing."

- Choose your words carefully. You can't take them back.

- See things from the other person's point of view.

- Don't assume you know what your partner is thinking.

- If you can't find a solution, agree to disagree.

Above all, treat one another with respect.

A soft answer turns away wrath, but a harsh word stirs up anger. (Sirach 15:1)

Jesus, our Redeemer, teach us to act with calm and grace in the face of disagreement.

Book Bonding

When Ptolemy Tompkins married his wife Rebecca, he moved into her tiny Greenwich Village apartment. Tompkins was struck by the polite, cautious silence he received from Rebecca's seven-year-old daughter, Mara—and by the number of books the mother and daughter had.

Tompkins, writing in *Guideposts* magazine, said he knew how Mara felt. "I had received a step-parent of my own back when I was Mara's age," says Tompkins. "I remembered how vigorously I tried to push this strange new woman out of my field of vision, at the very beginning."

Tompkins began carefully selecting new books to add to Mara's collection. With each one, he says, "I got to know her a little better—and came closer to feeling like I might really belong in her life after all."

Blended families present a challenge for all members. Seek out common interests and beliefs that may serve to unite the family.

As a mother comforts her child, so I will comfort you. (Isaiah 66:13)

Holy God, bless and assist families in their struggles to live and love together.

Going to the Chapel...With a Donation

Weddings are a time of joy, hope and promise. They are also a time of gift-giving—and the hopes that whatever we bring to the betrothed will be met with approval and gratitude. That helps to explain the proliferation of gift registries, which enable the happy couple to guide friends and family in their generosity.

A new trend is gaining momentum among soon-to-be-marrieds: *charitable* giving registries. Meghann and John of New York City created a wedding registry where gift-givers can make donations to organizations selected by the couple. For example, they chose groups like Safe Horizon, which supports victims of crime and abuse, as well as Improve Life Skills, which funds youth soccer leagues.

This way, the couple tailored their gift selections to align with their own personal convictions, and organizations that helped others in specific ways. What better way to start a life together?

Do not seek your own advantage, but that of the other. (1 Corinthians 10:24)

Lift us out of the misery that comes from self-centeredness, Father, and give us the joy that comes with generosity.

Sharing Yourself with God

Danielle Bean is co-author of the book *Small Steps for Catholic Moms*. She was recently a guest on the *Christopher Closeup* radio program and talked about the kind of relationship God wants to have with us, His children.

Bean compared it to her toddler's achieving some accomplishment and immediately wanting to share it with her.

She explains, "They don't consider the experience complete until you've shared it with them. That's the kind of natural relationship God wants us to have with Him—that no experience is complete until we've turned to God, whether it's a joy, a sorrow, a challenge, or a triumph."

Nurture your relationship with God every day. And turn to Him frequently to share a moment—and to say "Thanks."

Always and for everything (give) thanks in the name of our Lord Jesus Christ to God the Father. (Ephesians 5:20)

Eternal Lord, thank You for letting me share the joy of Your loving presence.

Clear the Field!

Finally getting around to clearing the clutter in your home? Thinking about how in the world you will dig out from under a lifetime of accumulation?

Clutter-clearing expert Barbara Tako offers tips to those at or near retirement to make a daunting task much easier.

First, Tako suggests that it's prudent to embark on such cleaning expeditions while you're healthy and able.

Second, label and write down who will inherit the stuff you care about. Leaving such decisions to family members later could lead to disagreements and confusion.

Finally, life stories are not clutter. Capture your "story" by writing down little-known facts about the items you do treasure, so loved ones receive more than just "Grandma's plate," but rather, a story rich with history and emotion.

Clearing clutter helps refocus the mind and frees energy for hobbies and relationships. Stop procrastinating, and clear the field!

There is great gain in godliness with contentment; for we brought nothing into the world, so that we can take nothing out of it. (1 Timothy 6:6-7)

Holy Spirit, free me from material encumbrances.

Giving Back, on a Global Scale

Dr. Alan Crandall, Chair of Ophthalmology and Visual Sciences at the John A. Moran Eye Center in Salt Lake City, doesn't just help heal patients in the United States.

For well over a decade, Dr. Crandall has been traveling to Third World countries to train doctors and staff to perform eye surgeries.

Dr. Crandall and his team, which includes an anesthesiologist and other doctors, visit impoverished nations and teach their doctors about the latest techniques and technologies in eye surgeries.

The team has carried out missions all over the world, from Brazil to Egypt to Tibet, to name only a few of the countries they've visited. The team provides all necessary supplies, and even pays for doctors to come to Utah to train under their supervision. Dr. Crandall says the work rejuvenates the doctors and inspires them in their daily work.

Funny how in giving, we receive.

How does God's love abide in anyone who has the world's goods and sees a brother or sister in need yet refuses to help? (1 John 3:17)

Help me grow in love and generosity, Prince of Peace.

Not Your Typical Commencement Address

American columnist, author, and political satirist Russell Baker has addressed a wide range of audiences on a variety of topics. But it was his 1995 commencement address to Connecticut College that struck many as his most poignant speech.

Instead of telling graduates to "go forth in the world," which Baker regarded as predictable and even boring, he delivered a decidedly contrarian message.

He listed "10 things to help you avoid making the world worse than it is." They include: smell a flower; listen; pick up a book; have some children; get married; and smile.

He also advised graduates to deflect negativity and doom. "When they come at you with that, give them a wink and smile…and as you stroll away, bend down to smell a flower."

How much of life is lost in the pursuit of a lifestyle? Life is short; avoid the naysayers and focus on what matters.

All wisdom is from the Lord, and with Him it remains forever. (Sirach 1:1)

Direct my thoughts to all that is holy, Creator.

Working to Fulfill God's Plan

On this Feast of the Ascension, the words of Deacon Greg Kandra offer a thoughtful reflection. As he wrote on his blog, *The Deacon's Bench:*

"In Matthew's gospel, before Jesus ascends, he tells the apostles, very simply, 'Go therefore and make disciples of all nations.' He urges them to baptize, to teach, to carry on the work that he has begun. But his first direction is so clear: 'Go.' The world is waiting. Act on what I have taught you.

"And the reading from Acts even challenges them. As they have watched him disappear into the clouds, two men ask them: 'Men of Galilee, why are you standing there looking at the sky?'

"The apostles were not supposed to spend their time staring nostalgically at the stars. There was work to be done.

"How will we fulfill that beautiful work today? How will we transform it into a prayer? How will we heed Christ's order to 'go'? How will we make the ordinary tasks transcend—and ascend? How can we raise our lives to God?"

Jesus came and said to them..."Go therefore and make disciples of all nations...And remember, I am with you always, to the end of the age." (Matthew 27:18-20)

Lord, help me fulfill Your plan for me.

Encouraging Teen Volunteerism

Like many of us, teens can be self-centered at times, but there are ways to break through and interest them in community service.

Psychotherapist Michelle P. Maidenberg says that "teens are thinking about careers, college, and what their future might look like. This is very challenging and just one of the reasons why they are so focused on their own world."

Teens can be motivated to help others particularly when the project focuses on something that already interests them. Perhaps a youngster considering a veterinary career would enjoy volunteering at an animal hospital. Another with an interest in culinary arts might work at a soup kitchen.

"Community service helps to instill a maturity when they take a step back to see the needs of other people," says Maidenberg.

The right key can unlock the desire to serve in anyone.

You do well if you really fulfill the royal law... "You shall love your neighbor as yourself." (James 2:8)

Jesus, our Savior, remind us to find You and serve You in each person we meet.

Mommy's Got Class

Whenever Bailey Osborne thought about quitting school, a look at her four kids would renew her commitment to college.

"I knew in my heart why I just couldn't quit," says Osborne.

For her and other single parents, higher education is the surest ticket out of poverty. One state study found that among households leaving the welfare rolls, those who pursued a college education earned more on average and were less likely to return to public assistance.

While Theola Moore, who earned her degree online, admits "it wasn't always easy," she feels she set a good example for her children. "I tell my kids that the word 'can't' is not in our family's vocabulary," she says.

Achieving our goals may, at times, require extra effort and even some sacrifice, but our success can motivate others. And that's a win-win situation!

Commit your works to the Lord, and your plans will be established. (Proverbs 16:3)

Be my strength, Lord, when I call for Your help.

The Nun Who Goes to Prison

Maryknoll Sister Maureen Hanahoe spends her days in prison. This, she believes, is a special call from God—something she has been preparing for since she entered the convent.

Sister Maureen spent 27 years in Peru working with impoverished women, promoting health care and building small Christian communities. She became fluent in Spanish, and learned much about the devastation that drug abuse and trafficking brings to nations such as Peru.

She returned to her native New York in 2003 and learned that about one-third of the inmates in local jails speak only Spanish. Now she spends her days with inmates like Samuel, a heroin addict, who took her advice to heart and entered treatment upon discharge. "He has really started a new life," says Sister Maureen.

Try not to judge anyone on face value, but offer help to any neighbor in need.

You guide me with Your counsel, and afterward You will receive me with honor. (Psalm 73:24)

Jesus, bless those who help prisoners in their path to reform and recovery.

Chefs of the Future

It's not too early to foster a love for good, nutritious food and an interest in cooking in your children. Consider these tips to encourage kids in the kitchen.

- Rethink your space. Store everyday tableware within reach, so that everyone can help set the table, etc.
- Let them be creative with food and table settings. Provide safe kitchen tools for cutting and chopping, and the materials to make napkin rings and other table accessories.
- Label leftovers, so kids can turn a tasty dinner into tomorrow's snack or lunch.
- Wipe out spills. Teach kids to clean up their own place at the table—and their cooking area as well.

Meal time should also be family time—a part of the day to nourish body and spirit.

The eyes of all look to You, and You give them their food in due season. (Psalm 145:15)

Bless the food we eat, Almighty Father; satisfy all who are hungry this day.

Beauty in Bloom

What makes a community beautiful? For 79-year-old Mary Savage, the answer to this question is simple—flower gardens. Every morning, Savage leaves her house in Pittsburgh, Pennsylvania, to transform vacant parking lots into colorful paradises of lush plants. Obtaining land for her gardens is no hassle for this determined "flower lady." She says, "If I see a site I want to garden and if the city owns it, I get a garden waiver."

Mary Savage's 31-year mission of planting gardens goes far beyond roses and tulips, however. To Savage, her gardening is both a hobby and necessity. "There was a lot of blight," Mary said of the littered lots before her transformative efforts.

Follow Mary's example and add a little beauty to your community today, even if it means just planting a simple row of flowers on your front lawn. Remember, God gave us this earth and it is up to us to care for it.

Long ago You laid the foundation of the earth; and the heavens are the work of Your hands. (Psalm 102:25)

Lord, help us to take pleasure in bringing beauty to what You have given us and, in so doing, to help bring beauty and joy to the lives of others.

Setting Up Supper

Elizabeth felt like crying every time she looked at him.

Her older brother Jack's marriage had fallen apart, and he was devastated. He moved back near their parents, but seemed to sleepwalk through every day.

One night the pre-teen found her big brother in the neighborhood market, totally unmotivated to make dinner for one. Elizabeth immediately left and ran down the avenue, finding Jack's friend in a nearby shop.

"My brother needs a friend," she told Jack's buddy, Ray, who immediately texted him an invitation to burgers at the local diner.

As we watch those we love suffer—no matter the cause—we need to watch also for the moments that we can help ease the pain.

Sacrifice and offering You do not desire, but You have given me an open ear. (Psalm 40:6)

Lord, I trust You are with me, leading me through the dark times.

Passing On Hope

Growing up in her native Kiribati in the Pacific (the former Gilbert Islands), Merieti Riiki was inspired by the dedication and commitment of missionary Sisters who taught her in school.

When she grew up, she said, she also wanted to "touch the lives of others with God's great love and the hope He gives."

Now a Religious Sister in her homeland, Riiki works with elementary school teachers to develop displays, songs, plays and prayers that awaken young minds to think more about children from around the world. Those activities, she says, teach young people they can and must make a difference for other children—and help them develop compassionate and generous hearts.

"How great to be able to pass on that hope to children today," Sister Merieti says.

Today, be a sign of hope for someone in need—or point another in that direction.

Have unity of spirit, sympathy, love for one another, a tender heart, and a humble mind. (1 Peter 3:8)

When I am fearful or afraid, send someone to me, Lord, whispering Your love and hope.

Ways to Say Thank You

Alta Ray received close to 100 blood transfusions in a two-year period. The treatments were successful in helping this California schoolteacher beat leukemia.

Although the hospital promised the donors they would remain anonymous, Ray still wanted to thank them. And she was able to do that with 11 of them, who agreed to meet her at the annual blood-donor-recognition lunch at the Ronald Reagan UCLA Medical Center. Those donors included one of Ray's three sons, and a man who lost his own wife to renal cancer and has donated ever since.

"Each time I received a unit of blood, I thanked the person emotionally, spiritually," Ray recalled. "But I never expected to meet them."

A thank-you—spoken or offered in prayer—is our best response to the blessings sent our way.

Give thanks in all circumstances; for this is the will of God in Christ Jesus for you.
(1 Thessalonians 5:18)

I see all the good You have sent my way, Father, and I adore You.

Aging Happiness

As we get older, there are surely things about us that reflect the passing years. We may not see or hear as well as we once did, or walk or run as fast as we used to.

But there is something that improves as we age—our happiness. A new Gallup poll has found that by almost any measure, people get happier as they get older.

"It could be that there are environmental changes," said Arthur A. Stone, the lead author of a new study based on the survey, "or it could be psychological changes about the way we view the world, or it could even be biological—for example, brain chemistry or endocrine changes."

No matter the reason, it's surely a plus-side of growing older. But no matter our age, the inherent goodness of God's great gift of life gives us all a reason to rejoice.

Is wisdom with the aged, and understanding in length of days? With God are wisdom and strength; He has counsel and understanding. (Job 12:12-13)

Divine Master, I offer You praise.

A Prayer for Unity

In order to help us achieve the unity to which God calls us, here is a special prayer to the Holy Spirit:

"When we are divided in our family, Holy Spirit, make us one.

"When wars divide us, Holy Spirit, make us one.

"When injustice and exploitation build barriers, Holy Spirit, make us one.

"When divisions beset your Church, Holy Spirit, make us one.

"When sin separates us from the Body of Christ, Holy Spirit, make us one.

"When we come to the final stage of our life's journey, Holy Spirit, make us one. Amen."

Families, workplaces, churches, and nations all suffer from divisions from time to time, some of which can lead to physical or emotional violence. We need God's help in order to bring healing to these situations. Be open to the Holy Spirit's loving guidance.

The spirit of the Lord God is upon me...He has sent me to bring good news to the oppressed, to bind up the brokenhearted. (Isaiah 61:1)

Help me to be a peacemaker, Holy Spirit.

A Sacred Charge

On May 15, 1868, John A. Logan, the Commander-in-Chief of the Grand Army of the Republic, established Memorial Day to honor the fallen members of the U.S. military. In his proclamation, he said words that still ring true:

"We should guard their graves with sacred vigilance...Let no vandalism of avarice or neglect, no ravages of time testify to the present or to the coming generations that we have forgotten as a people the cost of a free and undivided republic.

"If other eyes grow dull, other hands slack, and other hearts cold in the solemn trust, ours shall keep it well as long as the light and warmth of life remain to us.

"Let us...gather around their sacred remains and garland the passionless mounds above them with the choicest flowers of spring-time; let us raise above them the dear old flag they saved from dishonor; let us...renew our pledges to aid and assist those whom they have left among us—a sacred charge upon a nation's gratitude, the soldier's and sailor's widow and orphan."

Honor and pray for the deceased members of the armed forces today and every day.

Blessed are those who mourn, for they will be comforted. (Matthew 5:5)

Welcome the deceased into Your Kingdom, Father.

Comfort in the Crumbs

For Ann, the day started out like most of her days lately—filled with stress.

Her pre-teen daughter caused another morning scene. Once again, Ann left her home for work already upset.

At work, still in a fog, Ann went to get coffee in her office's break room. There on the table was a crumb cake—and Ann perked up. The sight of it immediately called to mind her dad, and how she would share this same cake treat with him. She recalled how they both would scoop up the crumbs that had fallen into the box with a spoon.

Ann sipped her coffee and ate crumbs, smiling at happy memories—the morning's drama pushed far into the background.

In our own lives, we can take comfort in thoughts of good times past. These can help overcome the passing moments of any day's difficulties.

My times are in Your hand...save me in Your steadfast love. (Psalm 31:15-16)

Send me Your strength, Gentle Redeemer, that I may live in hope.

Supporting Survivor

Sue Alexander was standing on a second-floor porch talking with two Haitian girls when the earthquake hit that country January 12, 2010. Helped to safety herself, the volunteer nurse's immediate action was to pray. She continued to do so as she used her medical supplies to care for the wounded.

After four days, Alexander was out of supplies, and she returned home to New York. "I had done what I could in the neighborhood as far as wound care," she explained. "I didn't want to drink water or eat food that other people needed so I left."

But, once home, Alexander continued helping the poor of Haiti through financial support. Prayer is also a daily priority for her, and she encourages others to assist ongoing relief work there.

All part of God's one family, we are called to love and help our neighbor—near and far.

O my God, I cry by day, but You do not answer...Yet You are enthroned on the praises of Israel. In You our ancestors...trusted, and You delivered them. (Psalm 22:2-4)

Although devastation and fear surround me, I put my faith in You, Lord.

Paintings for the Birds

"House hunting" for Barry and Lisa Van Dusen was more like "garden shopping." Twenty-five years ago, the Massachusetts couple went searching for a place that had plenty of room to plant gardens that would attract birds.

For Barry Van Dusen, it was not only a matter of pleasure—sharing, with his wife, a love of nature—but also a business priority. He's an award-winning bird artist.

After a quarter-century in that home, with two acres of bird-attracting gardens, Barry admits an "emotional connection" with his feathered subjects. "It's almost like painting your own family," he says.

We are all stewards of God's creation, called to celebrate and care for the life and beauty that surround us.

Then God said, "Let the earth put forth vegetation: plants yielding seed and fruit trees of every kind on earth that bear fruit with the seed in it." And it was so...And God saw that it was good. (Genesis 1:11-12)

I give You thanks, Heavenly Father, for the abundance of earth and sky.

Cat and Dog Connections to People

It's in the brain.

That's the reason humans are drawn to cats and dogs—and the answer to why they return the attachment.

Of all the brain chemicals, one turns out to be more important than any other. Oxytocin is the main ingredient in the complex chemistry of attraction between men and women. This chemical in all mammals' brains also factors into our connection with our pets.

Petting a cat, for example, raises the level of oxytocin in both parties. The person feels less stressed, and the pet, more trusting. And that same brain chemical has been found to help lower heart rate and blood pressure, thus helping to ward off heart attack and stroke.

Demonstrating care and concern for animals as well as for our family and friends is also soothing to the soul.

Who among all these does not know that the hand of the Lord has done this? In His hand is the life of every living thing and the breath of every human being. (Job 12:9-10)

Bless me, Jesus, with good friends and peace-filled days.

Don't Sink—Swim!

Former *American Idol* contestant Brooke White released an album called "High Hopes and Heartbreak" in 2009. The title reflects some of the struggles she's faced in her life and career. Yet when White was a guest on our *Christopher Closeup* radio show, she confirmed that she is ultimately a person of hope.

White told program host Tony Rossi, "In times when I have struggled and gotten real low, there's this point where I just want to give up. And somehow, there is always this part of me that just can't, that doesn't know how to do that. I really think I owe that to God and my family. At the end of the day, I don't know how to sink; I know how to swim."

When life's troubles get you down, call on God and the people who love you. Their strength can help you keep your head above water.

> **Do not worry about anything, but in everything by prayer and supplication with thanksgiving let your requests be known by God. And the peace of God, which surpasses all understanding, will guard your hearts and your minds in Christ Jesus. (Philippians 4:6-7)**

Merciful Father, hold me in Your comforting arms when problems surround me.

Would You Still Love Me If...

There's a wonderful children's book called "Would You Still Love Me If..." that we honored with a Christopher Award in 2011. Written by Wendy LaGuardia and illustrated by Patricia A. Keeler, it tells the story of a boy named Michael.

Whether he strikes out in Little League or earns a bad grade, Michael asks his mother if she still loves him despite his mistakes. She always assures him she does, then adds, "One day you will see just how special you are to me."

As Michael journeys from childhood to manhood, his mother's unconditional love builds his self-confidence and instills him with a desire to help others.

When Michael's mother is older and very sick, she wonders if she's too much trouble for him. He responds, "When you love someone, they can never be too much trouble. Now it's your turn to see just how special you are to me."

When our family members get older and need help, let's reflect God's love by treating them with compassion and concern.

Whoever does not provide for relatives, and especially for family members, has denied the faith. (1 Timothy 5:8)

Guide me in caring for my loved ones, Divine Master.

Harboring Hearts

When Yuki Kotani's father came from Japan to New York City for a heart transplant, she stayed by her father's side as much as possible, running in and out of the hospital after work.

The New York resident considered herself one of the lucky ones because she wasn't living in the hospital's waiting room, like other patients' families who couldn't afford a hotel.

Then Yuki met Michelle Javian, another daughter of a heart patient. The two created Harboring Hearts, an affordable housing option for heart patients and their families. They are starting small, helping one family at a time.

For instance, Harboring Hearts helped pay the rent, food and phone bills of a young mother from Trinidad whose twin three-year-old sons both needed heart transplants.

Their donor circles are small, but the lasting contributions come from Harboring Hearts' willingness to make others' lives easier.

How do we go out of our way to make other people's lives easier?

The second commandment is like the first: You shall love your neighbor as yourself. (Matthew 22:39)

Father, help us to serve others in Your name.

Not Buying Happiness

Here's an interesting fact: Happiness scales in the United States were higher during the Great Depression than they were in 2000.

In fact, one study suggests that while happiness increases for people who move from poverty into the middle class, gaining more money after that has little effect.

During difficult economic times, families are often surprised by the dividends of a simplified lifestyle. Try some of these ideas for yourself: Get what you need and have a picnic instead of a meal in a fancy restaurant. After all, family time is the most important thing. Invest in your relationships.

Acquiring things may fill up a house, but spending time with the people in your life fills up your heart—and it's free!

In every circumstance, it costs nothing to reach out in love and kindness to our neighbor.

To the one who pleases Him, God gives wisdom and knowledge and joy; but to the sinner He gives the work of gathering and heaping, only to give to one who pleases God. (Ecclesiastes 2:26)

You fill up my life with good things, Blessed Trinity, and love beyond all measure.

The Man Who Opened the Sky

William Gordon found himself in the position of trying to do the impossible. "We were young enough that we didn't know we couldn't do it," Gordon said years later.

But do the impossible Gordon did, building the world's largest, most powerful radio telescope. Completed in 1963 and situated in Arecibo, Puerto Rico, the project proved to be among the most useful instruments for probing the secrets of the universe.

Looking through the giant lens, researchers discovered the first solid evidence of neutron stars, the rotation period of Mercury, lakes on one of Saturn's moons, and details about the surface of Venus.

Encourage those around you to dream and imagine a world of endless possibilities.

The heavens are telling the glory of God; and the firmament proclaims His handiwork. (Psalm 19:1)

When I falter, strengthen me and send me Your hope, Paraclete.

For India, a New Era of Accountability

At the end of the 20th century, the Indian state of Bihar loomed as "an omen for what would happen to the rest of India under incompetent management," according to travel writer William Dalrymple.

Bihar was mired in government neglect, corruption and class conflict. Yet under the direction of Chief Minister Nitish Kumar, it has transformed. The economy grew 11 percent annually over the last five years; 4,200 miles of roads and 1,600 bridges and culverts were built. Tourism rose, while banditry and kidnappings fell.

How did this happen? There's a new insistence on accountability and competence which has bolstered the civil service corps and public projects, eliminated red tape and nepotism, and empowered local officials. By making law responsible to the people it serves, democracy now has a fighting chance.

One person in the right place, at the right time, can create amazing changes.

The righteous are bold as a lion.
(Proverbs 28:1)

Beloved Father, give us courage to take difficult paths, for our struggle may help create a brighter world.

Hunger in America?

There may be an obesity crisis in this country, but there's also a disturbingly high rate of hunger or food insufficiency.

An Agriculture Department report in 2009 showed that the number of Americans who lacked reliable access to sufficient food increased greatly last year.

While the problem may not be starvation, families of the working poor and unemployed often have trouble putting enough nutritious food on the table at times during the year.

There are many ways to tackle social problems, from national political action to local community efforts. Find a way to pitch in and help your neighbors in need.

"I have given every green plant for food." And it was so. God saw everything He had made, and indeed, it was very good.
(Genesis 1:30-31)

Show us how to assist those in our communities who lack the nutritious food they need for good health, Holy God.

Filling the World's Freezers

Diane Lang and her family were having a bad year.

The folks from Columbus, Ohio, faced one hardship after another. The couple lost their business. They also had to pay more than $20,000 in health insurance costs.

To cut down on food expenses, the family bought meat in bulk, stocking up the big freezer in their garage. Then one day, finding the freezer door open, they faced another loss—thousands of dollars of ruined food.

Lang wrote about their difficulties on her Internet blog site. A few days later, three readers showed up with food to restock the family's freezer—driving there from 400 miles away.

All part of God's family, we're called to learn and meet the needs of our neighbors next door and across the globe.

Bear one another's burdens, and in this way you will fulfill the law of Christ. (Galatians 6:2)

This day, I am ready, Paraclete. Send me to show Your love to Your children.

Lifetime Thank You

Growing up in Nigeria, Hyacinth Egbebo was awestruck by the presence of Catholic missionaries. "Someone who didn't know us came from a distance, to help us, to give us an education, and to offer us the love of God," he explains.

Now a bishop in his homeland, where Christians are a minority, he credits those missionaries with inspiring his vocation. "My priesthood remains an expression of gratitude to those missionaries," says Bishop Egbebo.

And, he adds, he's ready to work as hard as he can—as those missionaries did—to help others come to know the Lord's love. He says, "We are prepared to go where we are sent, and make Christ known in every possible way."

How do you say thank you? Loving kindness to others, demonstrated daily, is surely something all can be grateful for.

The Spirit of the Lord speaks through me, His word is upon my tongue. (2 Samuel 23:2)

My service to others is offered with thanks and praise to You, Blessed Trinity.

A Journey of Faith, a Lifetime of Healing

Without her strong faith in God, breast cancer survivor Heather St. Aubin-Stout claims she would have never been able to withstand the diagnosis and recurrence of the disease that had taken her mother's life. Yet even in the midst of the anguish and fear this cancer inevitably brought, the beacon of God's eternal light inevitably shone through.

"I saw Christ in all those family and friends that were there for me with a kind word, a listening ear," St. Aubin-Stout stated. "I felt wrapped in God's love even when I broke down and cried over my situation."

Heather, a mother of three, chronicled her experiences in a book entitled *Not My Mother's Journey*. Her motivation for writing it was to help others realize they were not alone in their suffering.

God looks on our struggles with a similar empathy. Remember, Jesus Christ experienced death so that we could be resurrected with Him in eternal life.

Then the Lord God will wipe away the tears from all their faces. (Isaiah 25:8)

Most Merciful Healer, grant us emotional and spiritual recovery.

Free for the Asking

Sometimes the best things in life truly are free. Jake Frost came to this life-affirming realization singing the ABC song with his 18-month-old daughter Liz. At Liz's request, Frost sang the simple tune over and over again while his ecstatic daughter plopped pieces of carrot into a pot of vegetable soup. What struck him so deeply about this moment was not only how much fun he and his daughter were having, but how little their enjoyment was costing him.

"Sometimes we as parents fall into the trap of worrying about what we can't give our children," Frost declares. "We forget you make a life out of what you have, not what you lack." Frost's advice to fellow mothers and fathers is quite simply to give your kids "what you have."

Give thanks every day for the priceless values your parents have bestowed on you over the years and strive to keep these ideals alive in your own families. Believe it or not, the best gifts you can give your children are often "free for the asking."

Rejoice always, pray without ceasing, give thanks in all circumstances; for this is the will of God. (1 Thessalonians 5:16-18)

May we give thanks for the simple joys in life, Jesus.

Feeling Beautiful Inside and Out

According to writer Kimberly Snyder, eating the right foods not only improves physical appearance, but also gives a much needed boost to self-esteem. "I believe the word 'health' is synonymous with the word 'beauty,'" Snyder said in *USA Weekend* magazine.

To find your own inner beauty through a healthy diet, here are some nutritional tips:

- Cut out the soda. Soda adds unwanted calories.

- Load up on red peppers. Red peppers are full of Vitamins A and C, which prevent cell damage and premature aging.

- Add fresh herbs. Herbs such as cilantro and parsley can help remove unhealthy toxins from the body.

- Less acidity, more alkalinity. Studies show food higher in alkalines is not only delicious, but produces shinier heads of hair.

- Count on kale. Kale is a powerful antioxidant and blood cleanser.

Remember, cleanliness is next to godliness, so keep your body healthy and clean. You'll feel more beautiful inside and out.

Take care of your health. (Sirach 18:19)

Lord, help us take care of our bodies, the temple of our souls.

A Soldier's Voice

When Theresa Sareo lost her entire right leg in a tragic accident, she felt isolated and alone.

The first year of her recovery coincided with the beginning of the war in Iraq. She saw U.S. soldiers coming back from that war with amputations just like she had.

While her heart broke for them, not wanting them to have to go through the life she was living, Sareo admits that seeing them lessened her sense of isolation.

But the New York City songwriter didn't end the connection there. Sareo began visiting wounded warriors at Army hospitals in America and in Europe. She even wrote a song, "Through a Soldier's Eyes," inspired by her visits. Those encounters, she says, "heal you and heal the other person."

Our own life experiences can speak to—and strengthen—another's heart. See who you can connect with today.

You have been born anew, not of perishable but of imperishable seed, through the living and enduring word of God. (1 Peter 1:23)

In times of trial, I call to You; lift my burdens, Lord.

Work After 50

Finding any job is challenging. But seeking and securing employment past the age of 50 can prove particularly daunting.

Mark Miller, author of *The Hard Times Guide to Retirement Security*, offers these five rules.

- Don't push prior work. Experience is good, unless it makes you sound like you know it all.

- Be the solution. Offer ways you can help solve an employer's particular challenges.

- Network. Seek out potential employers at conferences, through alumni groups, and through online networking sites.

- Keep skills up-to-date. Take a class or find a "reverse mentor"—a younger more tech-savvy person, for instance.

- Look the part. Update your overall appearance appropriately.

No matter our age, recognizing our God-given abilities and putting them to use for others makes the best of every day.

There are varieties of gifts...varieties of activities, but it is the same God who activates all of them in everyone. (1 Corinthians 12:4-6)

Holy Spirit, may my words and deeds this day give You praise and serve my neighbor.

A Blessed Life

Can a life cloistered away from society be joyful? Absolutely, if this is your vocation.

Even if the wider world might wonder how a life of perpetual prayer can be one of true bliss, the nuns at St. Michael's Adoration Monastery of the Poor Clares of Perpetual Adoration in Bangladesh clearly feel it. In a way, they are not really isolated from society and its concerns.

"We pray for everyone all over the world," says one nun in a *Maryknoll* magazine article. "People do not know that we are cloistered, or what we do, but we are praying for everyone: all the sick, all the dying, all the poor and all the persecuted throughout the world." The nuns also pray for missionaries, peace and justice.

Says another sister, "I love my vocation."

It's a wonderful blessing to fulfill your true calling.

You whom I took from the ends of the earth, and called from its farthest corners, saying to you, "You are my servant, I have chosen you." (Isaiah 41:9)

Grant me the determination to seek Your will always and everywhere, Divine Master.

The Bridge Club

Eight-year-old Justine Prince racked her brain for the perfect Father's Day gift for her dad. Then, one day, as she and her sibling drove across New York's most famous bridge, the answer came to her: her dad would receive the gift of seeing his two disabled children walk across the Brooklyn Bridge.

On Father's Day 2010, Kirk Prince, dad to twins Justine and Julian—both of whom have cerebral palsy—watched his children cross the bridge in honor of their father.

Moreover, two of his children's friends accompanied the twins on their trek. All four cope with physical disabilities, yet all made the 6,016-foot trip.

Says the elder Prince, "It shows you that everything is possible."

Anything is indeed possible with the support of family and friends. Offer your hand and heart to others whenever possible.

The Lord honors a father above his children, and He confirms a mother's right over her children. (Sirach 3:2)

Thank You, Lord, for the people in my life.

Prayer Sisters — and Brothers

The ad in the newspaper sought support for a child far away. It sparked a thought for Barbara Mangione. If you could financially adopt someone you'd never see, why not adopt others in prayer?

The Indiana woman decided to do just that. She chose Palestine, directing her prayers for an unknown woman there, hoping she would come to experience the power of God's love in her life.

In *St. Anthony Messenger*, Mangione wrote that as she prayed faithfully for the woman in that troubled area of the world, she discovered she was acquiring many of the same blessings—peace of mind and heart, deeper love of and from family. Mangione started to remember in all her prayers her "brothers and sisters" around the world, as well as those suffering from disaster, disease, violence and the like.

God loves each of us unceasingly as His unique children. We must love as God does.

Is it not written, "My house shall be called a house of prayer for all the nations?" (Mark 11:17)

Jesus Christ, Your goodness is beyond all measure. Remind us to love our brothers and sisters the way You do.

Caring for the Giver

When Laura Wetherington's husband, Gary, retired, the two planned to travel, volunteer and just enjoy life.

But Gary Wetherington's diagnosis of dementia changed those plans; now it would be all about caring for him. As the South Carolina woman struggled to help her husband deal with his illness, she came up with these caregiver "musts."

- A caregiver must go with the flow, being flexible to help avoid frustration.

- A caregiver must appreciate the small stuff, learning to find joy in life's everyday moments.

- A caregiver must be plugged in, staying informed about a loved one's illness and treatments.

- A caregiver must reach out, seeking help from family and friends.

In life's journey, each of us—caregiver or cared for—can count on the hope found in knowing we're loved by God.

May Christ dwell in your hearts through faith, as you are being rooted and grounded in love. (Ephesians 3:17)

When I feel defeated, Divine Master, send me Your strength and love.

Yesterday's Neighbors

On a stroll through some New York City neighborhoods, you may just be walking past the past—from 100-plus years ago, in fact.

In East Flatbush in Brooklyn, for example, the Wyckoff farmhouse, dating back to 1652, is next door to a music club and across the street from a carwash. The Alice Austen house on Staten Island gives visitors a glimpse into Victorian-era bohemia.

The Historic House Trust works to preserve some 22 historic houses in the city's landscape, offering related tours and workshops.

Examining the past, we find memories worth treasuring—and, at times, mistakes best avoided. Don't be afraid to look at your own life so that you can learn from yesterday and move into tomorrow with hope.

Forgetting what lies behind and straining forward to what lies ahead, I press on toward the goal for the prize of the heavenly call of God in Christ Jesus. (Philippians 3:13-14)

In all times, You are my hope, Holy Immortal One. I give You praise.

A Child's Tale for Change

In 1873, Mary Ellen McCormack's neighbors took action.

Those living near this severely battered child complained to city authorities. Her city caseworker, Etta Angell Wheeler, stymied by the lack of laws preventing parents from abusing their children, turned to an unlikely ally—the American Society for the Prevention of Cruelty to Animals (ASPCA).

Ironically, it was a lawyer hired by ASPCA founder Henry Bergh who took McCormack's case to the New York State Supreme Court. The attorney, Elbridge Gerry, won the case.

He then started the New York Society for the Prevention of Cruelty to Children, which would rescue thousands of battered children, create shelters to care for them, and help formulate laws to punish abusive parents.

Solutions to life's challenges may, at times, seem out of reach. But there's always hope to be found—sometimes from the most unlikely of sources.

Whenever we have an opportunity, let us work for the good of all. (Galatians 6:10)

Heal me, Merciful Father. I put my faith in You.

Sleep — It's Not Optional

Getting a good night's sleep means more than just feeling good the next day. It can mean the difference between a strong immune system and vulnerability to colds and diseases, among other benefits.

Experts say that getting seven to nine hours sleep per night can result in an array of health benefits. For example:

- Fewer colds and sniffles. According to the Journal of the American Medical Association, people who sleep less than seven hours per night are three times as likely to catch colds.

- A trimmer waistline. People who get seven to nine hours of shut-eye had an average body-mass index (BMI) of 24.8—that's nearly two points lower than the BMI of those who slept less. Why? Too little sleep can upset hormones that regulate appetite.

- Lower risk of heart disease and diabetes. Lack of sleep is associated with higher levels of stress hormones, which may raise blood pressure and elevate blood sugar levels.

Come to Me, all you that are weary and are carrying heavy burdens, and I will give you rest. (Matthew 11:28)

Calm my soul, Holy Spirit.

Where Grandparents are Role Models

At Chess Without Borders, grandparents serve as role models for young people.

The non-profit organization, located in suburban Chicago, matches seniors with elementary school kids to teach them the art of successful chess playing.

Its mission distinguishes it from other chess clubs, in that Chess Without Borders mobilizes kids with varying degrees of academic success, and from a diverse cross-section of ethnicities and backgrounds.

Another unusual aspect of the program: participants also engage in charitable projects within the community.

Grandmaster Yury Shulman runs the program, and attests to the devotion of the volunteers. "I have played chess all over the world, but I have never seen chess being used as a provider of service and philanthropy," he says.

Which of your talents could serve young people in their journey to adulthood?

We have gifts that differ according to the grace given to us. (Romans 12:6)

Help us develop our gifts as we mature and grow, Holy Spirit.

A Glimmer of Hope

In recent times, the Dominican Republic has been ravaged by poor conditions. Most of the campos, or villages, lack potable running water, electricity, roads, health clinics or functioning schools. Prospects are dim for the impoverished residents of this small, island nation.

Sister of St. Joseph Beatrice Barry has made it her life's mission to assist Dominicans, who are among the world's poorest people. She started the Inn of the Good Samaritan there, which provides a place of help, hope and care for the ill and dying. At the Inn, Sister Beatrice and her team look after the sick by providing simple meals, bandaging wounds, administering medicines and providing shelter until each guest is well enough to return home.

"I do what little I can," Sister Beatrice Barry says simply.

The "little" effort you make to help the needy may in fact be quite big to the recipient of your kindness.

All who believed...had all things in common; they would sell their possessions and goods and distribute the proceeds to all, as any had need. (Acts 2:44-45)

Help me live a life of service, Savior of all.

Facing Your Fears

Fears and phobias keep many people from living life to the fullest. But there is hope and help.

Dr. Tedd Mitchell describes three forms of the anxiety disorder known as a phobia and offers tips for treatment in his HealthSmart column in *USA Weekend.* "Some of the physical symptoms of phobias are sweating, racing heart rate, shortness of breath, lightheadedness and nausea," he notes.

A person with a specific phobia has an overwhelming fear of something in particular—for instance a dog, a clown, a thunderstorm or a boat ride. A social phobia entails an irrational fear of gatherings where we believe others are unduly judging or criticizing us; agoraphobia is the irrational fear of any public place.

Treatment depends on the particular problem and may include various therapies and possibly medication. Help is available. Don't be afraid to get it.

Do not fear, for I am with you, do not be afraid, for I am your God; I will strengthen you, I will help you, I will uphold you with My victorious right hand. (Isaiah 41:10)

Holy Savior, help me to trust You to always support me, no matter what happens.

Millennial Relativism

A recent survey asked Americans between the ages of 18 and 29, the so-called "millennials," about their attitudes toward morality.

When asked about the statement "morals are relative"—in other words, that there is no definite right or wrong for everybody—two-thirds of those participating said they agreed. When posed to young Catholics, the percentage rose even higher, to 82 percent.

How is it that so many in the millennial generation believe that there are no moral absolutes? Stephen Kent, writing for the Catholic News Service, says that "a place to start would be recognizing the need for a right relationship with God."

He believes that if people of any age want to strengthen their moral attitudes they must begin by strengthening that personal spiritual relationship.

Make sure you yourself are right with God. Read the Bible. Pray. And let God guide you in all that you do.

I have taught you the way of wisdom; I have led you in the paths of uprightness...Keep hold of instruction. (Proverbs 4:11,13)

Remind me to obey Your will in all things, Gracious God.

Honest Conversation

When Bruce Feiler received a cancer diagnosis, his first thought was for his twin daughters. While his wife and other family members would clearly care for the girls, he was worried that they would be without a father's guidance.

That led this author of *Walking the Bible* to seek out friends he admired, whom he asked to join a "Council of Dads" to mentor his young daughters. It brought him closer to these men as well, and taught him the importance of real friendship built on integrity and trust.

Many of us don't talk to our friends about why they're important to us. We don't tell them what it is we like about them, why we admire them. But maybe we should.

Telling our loved ones why they're special will brighten their day, and may just bring them closer to us. Try it.

Some friends play at friendship but a true friend sticks closer than one's nearest kin. (Proverbs 18:24)

Encourage me, Gracious Father, to speak honestly and openly with my loved ones about why they matter to me.

Lighting a Long Day

The bus full of weary workers crawled along in late evening traffic. It was the Thursday before the Fourth of July weekend.

Each person seemed locked in isolation. Two were reading, while several others texted messages on their phones. Another had a small laptop and intently worked on some job-related task.

Suddenly, as the bus crossed a bridge just before reaching its destination, the skies lit up from a pre-holiday fireworks display. Splashes of bright colors and showers of sparks illuminated the night. Suddenly the texting, reading and working stopped. Now all the passengers were united in awe, smiling and feasting together on the magic of that singular moment.

Every day is filled with tasks. Every once in a while, however, we need to stop, lift our heads, and see the wonder waiting for us.

Great are the works of the Lord, studied by all who delight in them. (Psalm 111:2)

You are awesome, Gracious God; giving us all good things.

The Rules of the Soul

One day, Father Joe Krupp was driving to a retreat in Michigan on country highways along with a friend.

On a particularly narrow patch, he got stuck behind a slow driver and began to tailgate her in hopes she would speed up. When his friend observed, "Joe, I think your anger is making her go faster," Father Krupp had a revelation.

"It hit me," he later said. "I'm driving on a sunny day with my best friend in the most beautiful state in the union and I'm complaining because we're going slowly. You know what it comes down to? I was not in control of the situation."

The priest realized that trying to control other people and the situations in which we find ourselves pushes God out of our lives. "It hadn't occurred to me how blessed I was."

Remember that God's love is a living force within your whole life.

Agree with God, and be at peace; in this way good will come to you. (Job 22:21)

Show us where our limits are, so that we may allow You in to give us grace, Great Mercy.

Squeezing in for a Song

The town of Molt, Montana, has a population of a mere 15 people. Yet, on most Saturday mornings, this little hamlet manages to pack a local café with more than four times its population. The draw? Music.

The Prairie Winds Café seats roughly 55 patrons and people travel from neighboring areas to fill those seats for the Bluegrass Saturday Breakfast. The music consists of not only bluegrass, but Cajun, Dixieland, and rock-and-roll. The bands play for tips and a home-style breakfast and lunch, showcasing their talents on mandolins, guitars, fiddles, and even horns.

Says one happy customer, "This, to me, is America. We've been here since 9:30 this morning and I just had the time of my life."

Simple pleasures can bring great joy. A kind gesture, a welcoming smile or time shared with neighbors can enrich our lives in countless ways.

David and all Israel were dancing before God with all their might, with song and lyres and harps and tambourines and cymbals and trumpets. (1 Chronicles 13:8)

Teach me to appreciate all moments of my life, Heavenly Father.

A Summer Prayer

On his blog *A Concord Pastor Comments,* Father Austin Fleming shared a prayer for summer:

"Good morning, good God! School's out, and kids are off on summer vacation...I remember such a time, 50 years or so ago, when summer had no horizon: a time and place as close to heaven as a young heart might imagine.

"Something in a child's summer joy comes, I'm sure, as a gift from You, O Lord: a taste of timelessness, a promise of perpetual play, a season of sun and unreasoned joy...But where did those summers fly, Lord?...Do I still believe in summer's promise of pleasure unending, unbending to calendars clocking each day, tick-tocking away the weeks of warmth?

"If I don't believe in summer, Lord, how will I believe in You or in heaven where summer's joy surely never ends, where summer's timeless stillness calms with peace all other seasons' grief?

"I offer you these months, my heart's July and August days: come summer with me, Lord; summer deep down in my soul; restore my faith in summer's time, in rest, in joy, in play, in You. Amen."

His steadfast love endures forever.
(Psalm 118:4)

Open my heart to the joys of summer, Lord.

Floods of Hope

When Pakistan recently suffered the worst flooding in decades, brought on by unprecedented rainfall, some 1,500 were killed; millions were left homeless.

Samuel Clement was among the relief workers helping in the aftermath. Together, he and others provided food, blankets, cooking materials and tents to more than 30,000 families. They also distributed medical and health information to more than 60,000 people, and nutrition packets to some 48,000 children.

But material aid is not all that these workers offered their brothers and sisters in their homeland. "Through our actions," explained Clement, "we have taken Jesus Christ to all—especially the hope He offers."

Our kind actions are most effective when joined to a faith-filled heart.

Why are you cast down, O my soul, and why are you disquieted within me? Hope in God; for I shall again praise Him, my help and my God. (Psalm 42:11)

Help me be a source of aid and comfort to Your suffering children, Heavenly Father.

Seeking Success

USA Today chooses an annual All-USA College Academic Team—20 students selected for their outstanding achievements in the classroom, in research, and as community leaders. Among the traits they share are the willingness to take risks and to think big.

One of the 2010 winners is Neha Deshpande, a biology major at Johns Hopkins University, who says: "Do things because you care, not for your résumé or to stand out or look good. Above all else, it should be your passion that shines through, and then everything else will follow."

Each student believes that the key to their accomplishments has been loving what they do. They insist that their passion drives their hard work and persistence, that it strikes the spark that keeps them moving forward.

Devote your talents and energy to the things you care about. Success is more likely to come to those who let their passion push them as far as they can go.

Know...and serve Him with single mind and willing heart. (1 Chronicles 28:9)

Holy Wisdom, help me discover my true passion, and grant me the courage to follow it as far as I can.

We Hold These Truths

The founder of The Christophers, Father James Keller, was an expert on the Declaration of Independence. He passionately believed in its words, "We hold these truths to be self-evident, that all men are created equal, that they are endowed by their Creator with certain unalienable Rights, that among these are Life, Liberty, and the pursuit of Happiness."

Father Keller also liked to point out all the references to God in the Declaration. The Founding Father's referred to "Nature's God," "the Supreme Judge of the world," and "the protection of divine Providence."

Father Keller said, "The Founding Fathers knew that the truths contained in the Declaration were based on an old doctrine...For thousands of years, despite persecution, defection, and obstacles of every sort, the Jews had kept alive the sublime concept that man has an eternal destiny, that he derives rights from his Creator, and that because of this he has solemn obligations to his fellowmen, in each of whom he should see a child of God."

Remember that God is the source of all human rights—and that with those rights come responsibilities.

Be faithful. (Revelation 2:10)

You are the source of rights, truth, and goodness, Father.

Seeing No Limits

Growing up around airplanes in North Carolina, Barry Hyde seemed destined for an aviation career. Securing an interview with a major commercial airline, that path seemed set.

Then tragedy struck.

Sitting in as a safety pilot on a test flight, he went down with the plane when the engines failed. Hyde suffered major head and internal injuries; he lost his left eye, and the sight in his right.

Hyde fought back, pursuing flying from a different direction—aviation safety. He earned a master's from Embry-Riddle Aeronautical University, the first blind student in the school's more than 80-year history. Today, Hyde is an aviation safety analyst with the Federal Aviation Administration. He encourages others to see his life as proof there are no limits to what we can achieve.

Sometimes we set our own ceiling on what is—or is not—possible. Instead, we should seize the opportunity in every moment.

The Spirit helps us in our weakness. (Romans 8:26)

Lord, this day I want to see Your love, Your compassion, Your peace.

The Man Who Put a Hole in His Shoe

When Italian winemaker Mario Polegato was attending a convention in Nevada, he found his feet suffering in the desert heat—until he cut holes in his rubber soles.

Back home in Italy, Polegato worked on his quick fix, and after years of research created Geox technology.

While most shoes hold sweat in, Geox shoes let the foot breathe via a perforated sole and a porous membrane that Polegato designed with the goal of keeping dirt and water out.

Now out of the family wine business, Polegato manages his Geox company, producing more than 20 million pairs of shoes each year, and selling them in more than 100 countries.

Following through on a good idea is just as important as thinking one up.

If any of you is lacking in wisdom, ask God, who gives to all generously and ungrudgingly, and it will be given you. (James 1:5)

Send me Your wisdom, Master, that I may act to help others.

Here Comes the Sun Power!

New York City has 1.6 million square feet of it—all of it ideal to collect solar energy, say experts in that area.

"It" refers to rooftop space which takes up about 20 percent of the city. Putting solar panels on those rooftops can provide half the city's energy, explains Dr. Richard Perez, a solar energy research professor at the University of Albany.

And if you add in parking lots, and zones around factories and highways, Dr. Perez feels you can increase potential power coverage to 100 percent. That would certainly relieve the stress on New York's overloaded system, lowering the risk of dreaded blackouts.

God has given us an abundance of natural resources that can serve us well—and that we must also protect.

And God said, "Let there be lights in the dome of the sky to separate the day from the night; and let them be for signs and for seasons and for days and years..." And it was so. (Genesis 1:14-15)

Our songs of gratitude are sung to You, Creator, for the blessings that surround us.

Coffee, Music and Faith

An open microphone and a Catholic nun. That's the formula that makes Paulinas Coffee House in South Florida work.

Sister Tracey Matthia Dugas organizes the monthly event at a Catholic bookstore in Miami. Musicians play original songs; others perform popular praise and worship tunes. Some read poems or tell jokes during the "open mic" night that is also broadcast via the Internet. Sometimes there are also special celebrations of birthdays and of the miracles of life, such as happened with the visit of a child from Samoa who came to the area for life-saving surgery.

Sister Tracey, a Louisiana native, describes the regular event as a "work of grace. God brings together just the right people and elements so that we get what we need."

Our deepest longings are known to our Lord. We just need to open our minds—and our hearts—to receive them from Him.

Do not let loyalty and faithfulness forsake you; bind them around your neck, write them on the tablet of your heart. (Proverbs 3:3)

Gather us together, Eternal God, that we may find faith and hope in Your love.

Walking Around the World

It can be done in England, France and Germany—even the United States. The shoreline, the countryside and city streets may be involved.

Walking clubs are increasing the world over, happy to show eager trekkers all the beauty and wonder around us. These groups also offer an appealing way to meet local folks and fully experience a region's not-in-the-guidebook charms.

Many options exist for such experiences, from signing on with a tour company specializing in such vacations to getting a map and going it alone. Tagging along with a local walking club is often the best option, providing access to a tested route, and sights and scenery only locals know.

No matter where we roam, we need always respect and preserve all in God's creation.

The earth is the Lord's and all that is in it, the world, and those who live in it; for He has founded it on the seas and established it on the rivers. (Psalm 24:1-2)

Bless the work of our hands, Father, as we steward Your creation.

Sisters, Smiles and Socializing

Want to "get happy"? Several studies point to certain factors for finding joy.

According to the British Psychological Society, people with at least one female sibling reported better social support, more optimism, and greater coping ability. Sisters also encouraged cohesion in families.

Smiling too is key, says a DePauw University study. Adults with the biggest grins in their college yearbook were up to five times less likely to be divorced decades later compared to those who looked less happy.

And finally, another survey shows the happiest people spend the most time with other people—away from the solitary situations promoted by TV-watching or web-surfing.

In the end, happiness is a choice—a daily decision to recognize and embrace God's loving gifts all around us.

> **Light dawns for the righteous, and joy for the upright in heart. Rejoice in the Lord, O you righteous, and give thanks to His holy name. (Psalm 97:11-12)**

> *I rejoice, Master, for You have given me all good things.*

Facing Unemployment

Losing a job can start an avalanche of other problems.

"When you don't have a job, especially months on end, it really causes people to lose a piece of identity," said one Catholic Charities worker.

More than that, if being out of work leads to the loss of a home, troubles multiply. Anne Severes of Omaha's St. Vincent de Paul Society says, "If you don't have a roof over your head, you're basically in trouble from the get-go. We're trying to keep people in their houses so they can at least continue to look for work and have a stable place for their mail. If you don't have a permanent mailing address, it's hard to get unemployment checks or social security checks or food stamps."

Says another counselor, "When someone doesn't have a job, it's not just that person's challenge, it's a community challenge."

Look around to see how you can reach out to neighbors who are out of work or in danger of losing their home.

For the people had a mind to work.
(Nehemiah 4:6)

Open my eyes to the needs of my neighbors, Jesus Christ.

New England Sweetness

When he took Ned Perrin's writing class at Dartmouth in the 1990s, David "Tig" Tillinghast didn't know he would carry on a tradition and become a New England maple producer.

"Ned introduced us to sugar-making so we could get away from campus and meet some real people and get our hands dirty, and have something to write about," Tillinghast said in *Yankee* magazine.

The Connecticut native moved to Vermont and studied the science of sugar-making. He also immersed himself in local history and sought out old-timers to learn about the craft. Tillinghast sees sugaring as a way to protect land and to be involved with local culture. Moreover, it offers the opportunity for him to live in a magnificent forest that has produced maple sugar for generations.

Look beyond your own community to see the wonder of the wider world that God created.

No good tree bears bad fruit, nor again does a bad tree bear good fruit; for each tree is known by its own fruit. (Luke 6:43)

You offer us so many chances to appreciate Your great and good creation, God of all.

The Benefits of Volunteering

Every day new people join the ranks of volunteers and learn the rewards of spending time helping others.

One of them is Californian Lisa Anderson, who mentors an 11-year-old girl whose father is in jail. "We go to the beach, hit the zoo, get manicures together or see a movie," she says.

Anderson knows about having an incarcerated parent. Her father has been in and out of prison for the past 25 years. "Even though I was an adult when this happened," she said, "it was still devastating."

Although Anderson often participated in charity fund-raisers, eventually she wanted to do more than just go to fancy dinners and balls. "I decided it was time to do something hands-on," she said. "I signed up for this mentoring program and promised that I'd work with this girl for a year."

Now she plans to stay involved as long as she can.

Who needs your help today?

For you need endurance, so that when you have done the will of God, you may receive what was promised. (Hebrews 10:36)

Spirit of Hope, guide my efforts at enriching the lives of others, especially children.

Good Idea? Pass It On

If you are a book-lover, your books can provide a memorable legacy.

After Edith Jean Simpson's aunt died, her uncle took the time to go through his wife's personal library and record each title. He then made copies of the list and sent it to their children and grandchildren. He wanted them to be able to select the books they would like.

"How thoughtful!" said a nephew. "Otherwise, my aunt's library might have gotten just a hurried look-through. Now, her well-loved books will find their way into the hands of family members who will treasure them too."

Any books left over will be donated to the public library.

What a wonderful idea! Moreover, we can even plan ahead for our own libraries by letting family members know that we would like to share our books with them or others.

We don't always recognize the value of the gifts we have to share. Don't underestimate what you have to offer.

Do good...be rich in good works, generous, and ready to share. (1 Timothy 6:18)

Spirit of Knowledge, guide my attempts to learn and to help others as well by enjoying and sharing good literature.

In God's Presence

Prayer is central to Christian life, writes columnist Father John Kiley.

For instance, the gospel of St. Luke shows Jesus to be a man of prayer who used it in many ways: as an expression of gratitude, in praise and adoration, and to petition His Father.

"Authentic prayer will lead the devoted believer to a superior experience of communication with the divine," writes Father Kiley.

St. Teresa of Avila defines prayer as a conversation with someone we know who loves us. Quite simply, it's the enjoyment of the presence of God.

Father Kiley suggests that if we are ill at ease while in church or when prayers are offered, it's because we "have forgotten how to pray, how to dialogue, how to converse with God."

Jesus prayed frequently not just out of duty, but because He enjoyed spending time with His Father. We can do the same.

Take delight in the Lord and He will give you the desires of your heart. (Psalm 37:4)

Teach me to pray, Jesus. Show me how to enjoy living in the Divine Presence.

Mom on a Mission

In many ways, Jonah Wood Weishaar is a two-year-old like any other in Brooklyn's Park Slope neighborhood. But unlike other two-year-olds, Jonah's life may be coming to a close.

He is afflicted with a rare genetic disease called Sanfilippo syndrome, in which missing or defective enzymes lead to progressive degeneration of the central nervous system. Most die before their teens, and there is no cure. But Jonah's mother, Jill Wood, is determined to find one.

Every day, when Wood wakes up, her routine is the same: "I light a fire under myself and say, 'What am I going to do today to save my child's life?'" Her efforts have led her to a doctor who wishes to do a study on this rare disease, but needs 10 children to do so. Wood has found four families with candidates, and is continuing the search.

When you are faced with the worst, persevere with hope and faith.

You have heard of the endurance of Job, and you have seen the purpose of the Lord, how the Lord is compassionate and merciful. (James 5:11)

Merciful God, when we feel that we have nowhere else to turn, remind us to take action—and trust in You.

Learn to Adjust Your Focus

The frenzied pace of life makes concentrating on just one thing at a time difficult for many young people.

So, it's no surprise that Attention Deficit Disorder diagnoses (and medications) are administered in great numbers. For those who prefer non-drug solutions, psychotherapist Jonathan Alpert offers these self-management tips that help train your brain to focus:

Use specific action verbs when planning things, for example, "Call Sam Smith at 3."

Review your calendar each evening so you can start to organize, in your mind, tomorrow's plans.

Stay focused on what the other person is saying. Give yourself visual and auditory clues to recall information.

If you lose focus when there's lots of activity, go to a quiet place and play soft instrumental music.

Do the things that you do best first. This ensures success early on and will motivate you.

Happy is the person who meditates on wisdom...pursuing her like a hunter, and lying in wait on her paths. (Sirach 14:20, 22)

Christ, my Lord, help us to clarify what's important in our lives—and what isn't.

Lost and Found

Forty years ago, Rudolph Resta carelessly left his wallet in a jacket, which was stowed away in an unattended coat closet on the second floor of *The New York Times* headquarters, where he worked in the promotions department. When he returned for the wallet later, it was gone.

The thief took the wallet containing cash, leaving behind credit cards and a few photographs. But the wallet contained other pictures that Resta assumed were now lost forever.

In February 2011, José Cisneros, a security guard at the now former *Times* building, discovered the wallet while investigating an empty space between an unused window and the masonry seal behind it.

When Resta, now retired, received his wallet back, his eyes teared up with gratitude. A picture of his now deceased father, one of his wife, and another of his young children, were once again in his possession.

Sometimes God sends us unexpected surprises.

Wait continually for your God. (Hosea 12:6)

Lord, thank You for all the reminders we have that our ultimate fulfillment is in You, and not in the things of this world.

A House Built on Fungus?

It's no secret that mushrooms, particularly those of the shiitake and reishi varieties, offer numerous health benefits for those who eat them. But Philip Ross, a California inventor, sees even greater possibilities emerging from these fungi.

Ross runs an organic farm outside Monterey, where he grows dozens of varieties of mushrooms in darkened shipping containers. What triggered Ross's interest were the thin, white root-like fibers that grow underneath the plants themselves.

Underground, these fibers form a vast network called a mycelium.

Ross discovered that while the mycelium doesn't taste good, once it's dried, it displays remarkable properties. It's nontoxic, fireproof, resistant to both mold and water, and traps more heat than fiberglass insulation. Pound-for-pound, it's stronger than concrete.

Some engineers believe the mycelium could be used in place of wooden beams in constructing homes. "It's not so far-out," admits Ross.

What wonders lie within God's creation!

O Lord, how manifold are Your works! In wisdom You have made them all. (Psalm 104:24)

Guide us in our respectful use of this earth, Father.

Victory or Death

In a single battle, the independence of the United States became a real possibility—six months after America declared itself free from British rule in 1776.

Despite America's self-declared freedom, its army was failing. Disease was rampant among soldiers who lost battle after battle. George Washington, commander-in-chief of the Continental Army, had little time to secure the nation's future.

On December 24 of that year, he called a meeting in Pennsylvania to discuss a raid on Trenton the following night. During the meeting, Washington scribbled on a piece of paper. It read, "Victory or Death."

Washington knew if his army lost this battle, the future of the fledgling nation would be imperiled. But the battle lasted a mere hour, securing a solid American victory.

Freedom comes with a heavy price. Many risked and lost their lives to establish this nation. Honor them and all who have defended America over the generations.

**Proclaim liberty throughout the land.
(Leviticus 25:10)**

Bless our nation, Great Father.

Making a Great City Greater

Portland, Maine, boasts an impressive arts, culture and tourism industry. One grand attraction is the Merrill Auditorium.

Inside, the Kotzschmar Organ takes center stage, all 50 tons of it. Built in 1911, the organ consists of 6,857 pipes, which rise like towers against the backdrop of the stage. Some say that its magnificent sound resembles an entire symphony.

The Kotzschmar was one of many municipally owned organs built in the early 20th century. Today, it's one of only a handful that survive. Decades of shrinking budgets, urban crises and shifting priorities have placed the arts in the back row.

In Portland, however, public support for the organ remains strong and the tradition of yearly concert series brings the majesty of the organ's rich tones to new generations.

The arts can keep a community connected, healthy and alive! Support music and art where you live.

The mountains and the hills before you shall burst into song, and all the trees of the field shall clap their hands. (Isaiah 55:12)

May Your Word be music to my soul, Lord God.

The Cycle (and Circle) of Life

Father John Tasto, OSA, knew he wanted to be a missionary, even before he entered high school. The priest attributes his focus to two sources: his parents, and the Benedictine sisters who educated him.

After his ordination in 1967, he studied theology in Mexico, as part of his plan to move to Peru and help the poor there. After 21 years in Peru, Father Tasto moved back to Mexico, where he's taught in Tijuana since.

In fact, some of the same Benedictine sisters from his Indiana grammar school stepped into his shoes in Peru, enabling him to return to Mexico.

Moreover, some of the girls Father Tasto taught in Peru went on to become sisters, and ultimately, to teach at Father Tasto's school in Mexico.

Life can be viewed as a cycle that goes 'round and 'round. What we give to others often comes back to us.

The commandments...are summed up in this word, love your neighbor as yourself...love is the fulfilling of the law. (Romans 13:9-10)

Open our hearts to Your love, Divine Master, so we can share it with others.

Public, Private or Parochial?

While some families are fortunate enough to live in a community with sound public schools, others are forced to seek private alternatives. Still others choose parochial education for their children regardless of the quality of the local public schools.

Leslie Baty from Salt Lake City, Utah, for example, is not Catholic, but she chose a Catholic high school for her daughter because she wanted God to be part of the teen's schooling. "She is receiving an incredible education. I feel she is a step ahead of her friends in public school," she says.

A Catholic school in Salt Lake City also attracted Mary Kavilia, who is a member of the United Methodist Church. "The school community is like a family to us," she says. "We are pleased with the spiritual and academic education."

A religious education—whatever the religion—can bring an added dimension of spirituality to a child's life. Support educational freedom of choice.

The teaching of the wise is a fountain of life, so that one may avoid the snares of death. (Proverbs 13:14)

Help parents, teachers, and administrators put children first, Lord.

One Youth Minister

On a Sunday morning back in 1994, Din Tolbert made his way to the altar of a small chapel in Queens, New York, wearing a blue suit from the Salvation Army. Although he was known by many as a shy person, he began to deliver his first sermon. He was 12 years old.

Since then, the Rev. Din Tolbert has been named the pastor of the very same church, the Allen A.M.E. Church, which makes an effort to include youngsters in its daily operations. In fact, young people run almost the entire Sunday service.

Says one high school student and worshiper at the Church, "Reverend Din makes the Word relatable to us. And to be trusted to handle money is edifying. Usually, people don't even allow teenagers to do that."

Young people are the future of communities, our nation and our faith. Make a place for the young at your house of worship.

For the word of the Lord is upright, and all His work is done in faithfulness. (Psalm 33:4)

Holy Spirit, cloak all children with Your love and comfort.

I'd Love To — Sort of

Diane Fitzpatrick is one of the roughly 35 million Americans who work predominantly from home, a trend largely fueled by a sagging economy and stubbornly high unemployment rate.

As if her situation weren't challenging enough, Fitzpatrick says that neighbors and friends who do work outside their homes erroneously believe she's on call to run their errands, pick up their kids and perform countless other favors during the workday.

"I have felt like the doormat of the neighborhood," she says.

So how does one say "No" gracefully?

Don't say yes right away; promise to check your calendar.

If you're booked, say, "I'm sorry, but I'm booked." Resist long explanations.

Allow people to return favors when you do say "yes." Ask them directly for help when you need it; it could help avoid resentment.

May the Lord of peace Himself give you peace. (2 Thessalonians 3:16)

Keep our speech honest but kind, Savior.

An Impromptu Gift—Of Life

Sixty-something security guard Ray Andrade and 37-year old nurse Merri Lazenby were longtime co-workers at an Illinois hospital who had never exchanged much more than a friendly "hello."

One fateful day in 2008, however, the two struck up a real conversation. Andrade revealed that he needed a potentially lifesaving kidney donation. On impulse, Lazenby offered one of hers.

Tests showed that Lazenby was a perfect match for Andrade's kidney transplant, and the operation went smoothly.

Lazenby doesn't think that she did anything special. "I'm a fixer," she says. "That's why I'm a nurse."

Indeed, people you least expect to help you may end up saving your life. Be kind to strangers as well as friends and loved ones.

Just as I have loved you, you also should love one another. By this everyone will know that you are My disciples. (John 13:34)

Encourage us to be a Good Samaritan for strangers in need, Gracious God.

Why Me?

Kate Braestrup's husband, Drew, planned to be a police department chaplain upon his retirement as an officer. "He was the one with the calling, the knowledge of Scripture, the faith that God was always there," she says. Braestrup, on the other hand, a self-described writer, intellectual and part-time skeptic, planned to write full-time once the couple's children were grown.

Braestrup and her husband's dreams were shattered, however, when Drew was killed in a car crash.

Shocked and grieving, Braestrup confided in a friend. "I've got to get out of this house, find a job, but I don't even know where to start," she cried. Her friend's suggestion took Braestrup off guard. "Why don't you become a police chaplain?"

Three months later, Braestrup entered the seminary. Today, she works as the Maine Warden Service chaplain, where she "bears witness to rejoicing in the gladness of the coming day," she says.

Pray for the strength to turn tragedy into triumph. Don't go it alone; reach out to friends, clergy, God for help.

The Lord is good, a stronghold in a day of trouble. (Nahum 1:7)

Comfort us in our sadness and grief, Counselor.

Consider the Alternative

Even in the U. S. where cars reign supreme, trains retain a mystique for hobbyists and travelers. They also provide commuters with an alternative to highway traffic congestion.

Over the years, railroads have had their ups and downs. They moved about 80 percent of passengers, goods and mail into the early 20th century, but after World War II more people chose to drive or fly. Concerned about keeping passenger trains in business, the government partly funded Amtrak in 1971.

Although by 1869 North America became the first continent to have a railroad from coast to coast, the U.S. now trails other countries in offering high-speed, efficient train travel. With pollution and crowded roads, many feel trains are the way to go.

In travel, as in all of life, choices are important.

Let us know, let us press on to know the Lord; His appearing is as sure as the dawn. (Hosea 6:3)

Help me to make all the choices of my life wisely, Holy Paraclete.

Fulfillment of a Promise

Sister Ann Terese Dana admits that throughout most of her early adulthood, she "prayed mostly in the face of tragedy, instead of turning to God in the first place."

She prayed fervently when her first husband died when she was just 25. She later remarried and promised God that someday, given different responsibilities and more time, she'd serve Him more. She didn't know that at age 57, she would be taking her vows to become a nun.

"My second husband died when I was 48, after 20 years of marriage, and I had to decide what to do with the rest of my life," Sister Ann says. Once marital and childcare responsibilities waned, she knew it was time to fulfill her promise. She began training with the Benedictine Order, and within a few years took her final vows to become a religious sister of the Missionary Benedictine Sisters.

"It all comes back to answering God's call and our trust and faith in Him," she says.

What does "serving God" mean to you?

Commit your work to the Lord. (Proverbs 16:3)

Encourage us to be holy in our daily lives, God.

Angel in Hiking Boots

Some angels give us comfort in times of adversity. Still others may just happen to have an extra knee brace for someone suffering from a painful injury at the Grand Canyon.

As recounted by columnist Joan Wester Anderson, experienced hiker Tammy Kline was both surprised and alarmed when her knee started throbbing while climbing in the Grand Canyon. She began to worry when the afflicted area still hurt the next morning, the day she and her husband, Rich, were to continue their climb up one of the Canyon's mountains.

"I prayed all night that God would help me find a way out," Tammy said. "This trip had been Rich's dream for as long as I could remember."

God answered Tammy's prayer in the form of a hiker named Tom who had an extra compression knee brace that enabled her to complete the eight hour trek to the top of the Grand Canyon.

Look to Tammy's example and pray to the Lord at all times, especially when you are in greatest need of His help.

When the righteous cry for help, the Lord hears. (Psalm 34:17)

Jesus, help us to trust You to answer our prayers.

Changes for the Better

In a forgotten town in the Dominican Republic called "the Batey," hundreds of migrant Haitian families dwell. They moved to this area because they were promised jobs by the local sugar industry. However, poor business practices and corruption took its toll and the sugar business failed. The Haitians found themselves out of jobs and in desperate need of outside assistance.

In June 2011, temporary help arrived in the form of parishioners from Our Lady of Good Counsel Church in Pompton Plains, New Jersey, and 10 DePaul Catholic High School seniors. In addition to rebuilding the Batey's dilapidated huts and helping in a local medical clinic, they brought the gifts of song and happiness to disadvantaged children in the Batey.

DePaul student Gina Glenbrowski said, "I wanted to change people's lives, but instead, my life has been changed."

Reach out to the poor, and change a life for the better. You may also find yourself positively changed.

They have distributed freely, they have given to the poor; their righteousness endures forever. (Psalm 112:9)

Jesus, help us to remember that charity begins within each one of us.

A Summer Well-Spent

As the end of summer looms ever closer and back-to-school sales begin, fashion columnist Marilyn Wetston has a list of practical do's and don'ts for the savvy consumer:

- Do check your closets first. See what's wearing out and where you need to fill in.

- Don't overspend or buy things solely based on a clearance price. Take into account fit, lifestyle and comfort.

- Do remember the cost-per-wearing rule. Consider well-priced, high quality items that can be worn for seasons to come.

- Don't get carried away. Set a budget and stick to it!

Be sure to share what you can no longer use with others who could benefit. And remember to spend your money wisely and well no matter what the purchase.

Be on your guard against all kinds of greed; for one's life does not consist in the abundance of possessions. (Luke 12:15)

Help me see clearly what I have and what I need, Jesus.

Lunch Lesson

Maggie and Eddie had been fighting for weeks. Troubles with their oldest son and financial issues with Eddie's small business filled their time together with snippy exchanges and constant stress.

One day, Maggie met some business colleagues for lunch. As the group chatted, one woman mentioned her husband's illness. "We're fighting this cancer together," the woman said.

On hearing that story, Maggie found herself thinking of her own marriage. She and her husband were fighting too—but against one another. How much easier it would be, she thought, if she and Eddie faced their struggles together, loving and supporting one another through the difficulties.

While the group finished lunch, Maggie texted her husband a three-word note: "I love you." He responded immediately with the same message.

Life is filled with struggles. But burdens are lightened when we have company to help us carry them.

My yoke is easy, and My burden is light. (Matthew 11:30)

I come to You, Lord, when I am weary. Help me find rest.

A Door and a Smile

For almost half the century that the Plaza Hotel has been open in New York City, Ed Trinka has been at the door—and smiling.

"That's what it's all about, being in front and making everybody happy," says the Plaza doorman. "To me, anybody that comes in there is a VIP."

When Trinka graduated from high school, his father, who was a garage manager at the hotel, told him to apply for a job there too. One day, when a doorman called in sick, Trinka got his chance. "They put the hat and coat on me," he recalls. "I got outside and started working."

Every task should be carried out in joy, a celebration of the good we can do for ourselves and those around us.

A cheerful heart is a good medicine, but a downcast spirit dries up the bones. (Proverbs 17:22)

In all I meet this day, Lord, help me to see and welcome You.

Picturing Food

Making food look perfect was once the priority for food stylists and photographers. Today's challenge—make food messy!

"People are interested in small butchers, artisan producers, farmer's markets—a more handmade look," explains Alison Attenborough, a New York-based food stylist.

Others feel the trend to make food look natural is intended to get people to buy the product, go out to eat or make a recipe. "It might enable us more to put ourselves in the picture," says Brian Wansink, director of the Food and Brand Lab at Cornell University.

Often life is less than picture-perfect. But even in the disarray and difficulties we sense the presence of God's healing love.

God is a God not of disorder but of peace. (1 Corinthians 14:33)

Send Your Spirit, Lord, to renew and restore all things.

God and the Gold Medalist

During the 2000 Summer Olympics in Sydney, Australia, Laura Wilkinson won the gold medal in platform diving a few months after she had broken her foot in a training accident. She credited her success not just to hard work and dedication, but also to the guidance she's gotten from her Christian faith—a faith she had drifted away from for a while.

As a guest on our *Christopher Closeup* radio show/podcast, Wilkinson recalled losing two people who were very close to her in 1997. She felt lost, consumed by fear, and even started getting disoriented in the air while performing dives.

Then, Wilkinson experienced a revelation. She said, "I realized what I was missing. I didn't know what God wanted to do with my life but I knew I needed Him to fix it and...to be the center of it and to put my pieces back together...I actually rededicated my life to Him in the middle of a diving meet. The way it's intertwined has really made me love the sport because God used it to bring me back to Him."

When you feel as if your life is broken into pieces, ask God to help make you whole again.

Endurance produces character...and hope. (Romans 5:4)

Heal my brokenness, Father.

Gazelle or Lion, Just Keep Moving!

In his book, *Once Upon A Time in Africa*, Maryknoll Father Joseph Healey offers stories from Africa, where he's served as a missionary for many years.

"These stories tell of compassion, conversion, forgiveness, grace, joy, mercy, peace, reconciliation, repentance and unity," he writes in the introduction.

One tale talks about the morning thoughts of a lion and a gazelle. Every morning in Africa, when a gazelle wakes up, it knows it must run faster than the fastest lion or it will be killed. Every morning in Africa, when a lion wakes up, it knows it must outrun the slowest gazelle or it will starve to death. It doesn't matter whether you're a lion or gazelle, the story ends, when the sun comes up, you'd better be running.

In our daily lives, we need also to keep moving. Spread God's love around as you do.

Discipline always seems painful rather than pleasant at the time, but later it yields the peaceful fruit of righteousness to those who have been trained by it. Therefore lift your drooping hands and strengthen your weak knees, and make straight paths for your feet. (Hebrews 12:11-12)

Help us run the race of life successfully, Lord.

Crafting Music

At first glance, the title of a recent exhibition at New York City's Metropolitan Museum of Art—"Guitar Heroes"—might call to mind some favorites among rock's legendary players.

But the museum show wasn't about the performers, but rather the creators of the instruments. Organized into two parts, the first went from string instrument-makers in 17th-century Naples to Italian immigrants producing guitars and mandolins in New York in the late 19th and early 20th centuries.

Part two offered lovingly made instruments from 1923 on. The "heroes" this time were three craftsmen known for producing some of the most sought-after jazz guitars of the last seven decades—John D'Angelico, James D'Aquisto and John Monteleone.

The exhibition also gives nod to the other side of the story, featuring videos of famed music-artists playing the creations of these craftsmen.

In life, as in music, cooperating with the Creator can produce perfect harmony.

Live in harmony with one another. (Romans 12:16)

I sing Your praises, Lord, for You send all good things my way.

Family Time

These days, many families become stressed because they are so busy. They have little time for pleasures they once enjoyed.

In the Kuehl family, Dad's a cop, Mom's a paramedic and there are three teens. They needed to de-stress and asked Kelee Katillac, an artist and creative therapist, for help.

"I started by asking 'What creates peace in your home?' They answered: teamwork, showing affection, honesty, creativity and...scuba diving!" says Katillac. They loved diving and saw the ocean as a place to reconnect.

"We just need some creative help in getting to know and understand each other all over again," says Mom, Bobbie Kuehl.

Katillac guided the family in jointly creating a glass-topped coffee table collage with soothing images of the sea, including a collage of underwater photos of family dives.

Make time for fun in your family life.

Deal kindly with my family. (Joshua 2:12)

Blessed Trinity, show my loved ones and me how to get the most out of our time together.

The Fountain of Youth?

Dr. Daniel G. Amen believes in the great importance of the mind and body connection.

According to Dr. Amen, the author of *Change Your Brain, Change Your Body*, "Chronic stress leads to increased appetite and abdominal fat" as well as to decreased sleep and prefrontal cortex function—"making you more prone to bad decisions." He continues, "Exercise boosts blood flow to the brain and increases a chemical which enhances cognitive ability. It's a fountain of youth for your brain."

If your mind is troubled you might be sleep-deprived, irritable or experience heart, gastrointestinal, and skin issues. What's the doctor's prescription for utilizing your brain power to help keep you fit?

"Sleep, exercise, a good vitamin-D level, positive thinking, and a brain-healthy diet with omega-three fatty acids all promote weight loss with lasting results," says Dr. Amen.

Something to think about—for your health's sake.

Heal me, O Lord, and I shall be healed; save me, and I shall be saved. (Jeremiah 17:14)

It's so easy to pigeon-hole our well-being of mind from that of our body. Jesus, help me to look after my whole self.

Small Gifts Making A Difference

The executive director of the St. Vincent DePaul Society in Omaha, Nebraska, appreciates the value of small things.

When an anonymous gift amounting to 22 cents arrived in the office, Anne Severes wrote about it in the *Catholic Voice,* newspaper of the Omaha Archdiocese. "What is the point of sharing 22 cents with an organization that needs hundreds of thousands of dollars to meet the most basic needs of those who seek its help?" she asked. If this was the only spare money the donor had, then sharing it was the very definition of stewardship, she writes—"operating for the greater good and planting seeds of hope."

In Severes' house, they use mustard seed to flavor large pots of spiced lentils. "The taste is extravagant," she writes, "and the cost is almost nothing."

Small donations add up to great generosity.

With what can we compare the kingdom of God...? It is like a mustard seed, which...is the smallest of all the seeds...yet when it is sown...becomes the greatest of all shrubs. (Mark 4:30-32)

Let me never discount the value of a penny or a mustard seed, Gracious Lord. And let me be generous to all.

Change, A Constant

Today's new media is shaking things up.

Long-established television producers, newspaper publishers and music-industry executives find themselves facing new challenges from all over the digital landscape.

This isn't the first time technological change has forced "old media" to adapt, writes Terry Teachout in the *Wall Street Journal*. It happened more than 60 years ago. In early 1949 network radio was still the dominant mass entertainment medium. There were about 85 million radios in use in America and fewer than two million television sets. But by the end of the year, more and more Americans were turning on to TV.

Teachout thinks today's media moguls can learn a lesson from this. They must be willing to "grapple with the challenge of the new media."

Change is often difficult, but since it's a human constant, learning to cope would be wise.

The grass withers, the flower fades; but the word of our God will stand forever. (Isaiah 40:8)

Eternal Paraclete, help me to respect the past, live in the present and welcome the future because time and eternity alike are Yours.

Taking Lessons from Tragedy

In contemplating his cousin's untimely death in an industrial accident, Father Ron Rolheiser recognized the profound pain it caused, but also knew that the family had consolations.

"His last days had been good; his last touches had been warm," Father Rolheiser wrote. His cousin had recently spent time with loved ones and parted on peaceful terms with everyone. His job was loading railroad grain cars, the priest wrote, and he died "doing his job."

While we are all mortal, Father Rolheiser says this should not make us fearful, morbid, timid about life, or guilty about enjoyment. "Conversely," he continued, "it is not meant to drive us to hedonism because life is short and unpredictable." The lesson, he said, is to "live prudent lives, care for our health and safety, and, if we have faith, we can pray for God's protection and providence."

Make peace with those around you and let loved ones know how you feel about them.

Death has been swallowed up in victory. Where, O death, is your victory? Where, O death, is your sting? (1 Corinthians 15:54-55)

Don't let me fear my mortality, loving Father, but rather celebrate the life You have entrusted to me.

A Horse for Grandpa

There are many expressions of love. When Randy Vogt was a boy, his grandfather shared with him his love of horses and racing.

"Grandpa seemed to know everybody (at the track) even if he didn't," Vogt wrote. He was also careful not to bet too much or in any way risk family finances. Vogt remembers his grandfather as an optimistic man who said things like "Be kind to everybody" and "It's nice to be nice."

Grandpa even took the young Vogt to see the house of jockey Ron Turcotte, who rode Secretariat to the Triple Crown in 1973.

One day, Vogt decided there ought to be a horse named in his grandfather's honor. He finally got it done by winning a contest to name a filly. The name: One for Grandpa.

It's good to know there are people who have a passion in life and share it with others.

How good and pleasant it is when kindred live together in unity! (Psalm 133:1)

Gracious God, bless me with a deep love for my family and friends.

In Awe, Both Then and Now

Wall Street Journal writer Joe Morgenstern was just a child during World War II. But he says that he "followed the European and Pacific campaigns with breathless excitement, and little or no comprehension of the heroism and horror behind the headlines, radio broadcasts, newsreels and Hollywood war films."

Years later, while reading a book by famed author James Michener, who had been stationed in the South Pacific, Morgenstern felt compelled to journey there in person.

While Morgenstern admired the beauty of the area, he found that the trip stirred a plethora of old memories and images of the war. "I never expected to see what I did," he says, adding that he gained "a sense of awe at the scale of our undertaking during World War II."

Honor and respect the men and women in our military who put their lives on the line.

How the mighty have fallen, and the weapons of war perished! (2 Samuel 1:27)

Lord God, remind us that patriotism can take many valuable and honorable forms.

When Jesus Lived

A first-century house recently discovered in Nazareth has people excited because it's the first one found there from the time of Jesus.

"The ruins," Auxiliary Bishop Giacinto-Boulos Marcuzzo of Jerusalem said, "were not destroyed during history. We don't know why but certainly there is a reason that house was kept safe."

Yardena Alexandre, excavation director at the Israel Antiquities Authority, said the discovery was important and provides new information about how the people lived: "The building that we found is small and modest and it is most likely typical of the dwellings in Nazareth," she said. It's not inconceivable that Jesus played near the dwelling as a child.

Some wonder who lived in that ancient house, in the same village where it was revealed to Mary that she would conceive a Child, "the Son of the Most High." It remains a mystery, for now.

You will conceive in your womb and bear a son, and you will name him Jesus. He will be great, and will be called the Son of the Most High. (Luke 1:31-32)

Open our hearts to Your tremendous love for each of us, Holy God.

A Regular Guy

William Herz has been eating at the same New York City restaurant for 77 years.

Since he was 16, Herz has dined at the famous Sardi's in Manhattan's theater district. That included a time when he performed on Orson Welles' panic-spreading radio broadcast of "The War of the Worlds" in 1938.

These days Herz, who has been an actor, stage manager, casting director and ticket agent, eats at Sardi's about twice a week. Throughout his lifetime there were many dinners and lunches, and celebrations—like his parents' 50th wedding anniversary and his dad's 95th birthday.

"I go to other restaurants, but I don't feel at home in other restaurants," he said.

Finding a place to feel welcome is a blessing. Creating such places for others is a worthy goal.

For I was hungry and you gave Me food, I was thirsty and you gave Me something to drink, I was a stranger and you welcomed Me. (Matthew 25:35)

I look to make You known to others, Lord of life, in the many moments of this day.

Staying a Samaritan

Michael Starks died at 18 from alcohol poisoning during a fraternity hazing ritual in 2008.

At least five other students knew Starks needed help, but they were afraid of getting in trouble and did nothing.

To put an end to such non-action, Starks' family is working to get their Utah state legislature to pass a "Good Samaritan" law to limit prosecution against someone who comes to the aid of a person experiencing a drug or alcohol emergency.

The family is busy collecting the signatures needed to support such legislation.

"What we are trying to do is endorse this idea of social responsibility," says George Starks, Jr., Michael's older brother. "This goes to the roots of our faith," he continues. "We are our brother's keeper."

Another person's need can be our call to action.

What does the Lord require of you but to do justice and love kindness. (Micah 6:8)

In my neighbor, help me to see You, Divine Master.

Serious About Clowning Around

As a child, Laurie Michelman regularly attended the circus with her siblings and her parents. "The clowns were my favorite part," recalls the New York attorney and college professor.

When her mother became gravely ill, Michelman began to reevaluate her life's goals—and revisit her childhood dream of being a clown. After a weeklong program, focusing on applying makeup, juggling and balancing, Lou-Lou Lollipop the clown was born.

Michelman's experiences in hospitals with her dying mother gave Lou-Lou a focus. She would become a volunteer hospital clown, working mostly with children.

"I teach them magic tricks and take them, for a few moments, to a happier place," says Michelman. "Laughter really does have healing power."

Every moment has the potential for joy—including being happy for God's generous gift of life.

You show me the path of life. In Your presence there is fullness of joy. (Psalm 16:11)

You are our strength, Divine Master, and the source of our joy.

Helping in the Kitchen

When the call came to help St. Mary's Church in Frankfort, Indiana, raise money for its building fund, churchgoers, particularly members of the Hispanic community, started cooking.

Volunteers donated everything from food to paper goods, then cooked and cleaned for a series of Mexican feasts. The average collected at the well-attended events was $450 to $600. That assistance goes a long way to pay for much-needed repairs on the old church.

Father Chris Miller, the pastor, calls the dinners "a beautiful act of thanksgiving" for the presence of the church in the community. One woman sees the effort as "giving back to God" for His blessings and paying tribute to their heritage.

"Someone here before us came along and built the church," said Marilu Castillo. "So now it's our turn to do what we can."

Each new day, give prayerful thanks for the love and blessings of so many yesterdays.

What shall I return to the Lord for all His bounty to me? I will lift up the cup of salvation and call on the name of the Lord. (Psalm 116:12-13)

Loving Father, strengthen me to face each day.

Bird Is His Word

Jay Holcomb spent much of his life rescuing birds. He started as a volunteer, and eventually became director of a California-based bird rescue and research center.

There he developed the search-and-rescue procedures that were used to treat birds affected by the Exxon Valdez oil spill in Alaska in 1989. He was called to the same task in Louisiana, after the Gulf Coast oil spill in 2010.

The cleaning process takes about an hour, Holcomb says, noting that dishwashing detergent works best. Birds are moved from bath to bath until they're clean, and are then dried with pet-grooming driers. He and his team took care of some 1,600 birds just during the Alaskan oil spill.

When a crisis happens, in our world, neighborhood or family, each of us is called to use our God-given gifts to make a difference.

Yours, O Lord, are the greatness, the power, the glory, the victory, and the majesty; for all that is in the heavens and on the earth is Yours. (1 Chronicles 29:11)

You gave us the beauty of nature, Divine Creator. May I always protect and preserve it.

Simple Gifts

When Kristen Sellan was a high school freshman in Columbus, Ohio, her grandmother died.

Wanting to do something to honor her memory, the young teen organized a group called Cuddles from Kristen. Volunteers make blankets and deliver them to the local Ronald McDonald House, a charity that offers care and assistance to sick children and their families.

A blanket seems like such a simple gift, but these cozy coverings let those in need know that they are remembered; that they are cared for; that they are loved.

No one needs vast resources or extraordinary abilities to make a difference. Using only your own talents and skills, you can change lives.

The hard part is turning our attention from ourselves to others. Ask God to help you, and then you, too, can start making a difference.

Those who are generous are blessed, for they share their bread with the poor. (Proverbs 22:9)

Help me to use my talents for others, Father of all.

Raising Rocket Scientists

In our increasingly technological world, "speaking science" is a necessary requirement. And America's first woman in space, Dr. Sally Ride, advocates encouraging children, especially girls, to embrace the subject.

"Science is exciting!" Ride says. "It surrounds us daily in the forms of technology, medicine, energy, environment, even the food we eat."

She credits her parents for encouraging her own passion for the subject, and offers these tips for other families to do the same.

- Encourage and reward. Make getting an "A" on a chemistry test as important as winning a soccer match.
- Take a family field trip. Go to an aquarium, science museum, or botanical garden.
- Stay current. Use current events to start a conversation about how science affects our daily lives.

Knowledge of any kind can improve our own lives, and help us to help others.

The wisdom from above is first pure, then peaceable, gentle, willing to yield, full of mercy and good fruits. (James 3:17)

Lord, You know my heart. Calm my fears and increase my joy!

Wash That Fruit — Maybe

In the plant world, "beauty products" are the dozens of chemicals that farmers use to fend off attacks from insects to fungus. The more vulnerable plants need many more chemicals.

In order to help in deciding when organic produce would be healthier, and when conventional produce is just fine, the Environmental Working Group publishes two lists—the "Dirty Dozen" and the "Clean 15."

Among the "Dirty Dozen" fruits and vegetables that get treated with large doses of chemicals (so buying organic is best) are strawberries, apples, celery and bell peppers.

The Clean 15 (so non-organic is just fine to buy and eat) include avocado, asparagus, mangoes and watermelon.

As we grow, in body and spirit, we too need protection. The best defense for our everyday needs is a healthy dose of nurturing love.

Since we have a great priest over the house of God, let us approach with a true heart in full assurance of faith, with our hearts sprinkled clean from an evil conscience and our bodies washed with pure water. (Hebrews 10:21-22)

Shower me with Your love, Lord.

Teaching Help

Once she got it, Roseann Brennan wanted to go into landscape and floral design. With hers, Maurisa Charles would be set to start college.

Both women prepared for "it"—the GED or high school equivalency diploma—at the School Sisters of Notre Dame Educational Center in Queens in New York City.

The Catholic nuns also teach English, and often bring in speakers to help the women deal with problems that are all too common in their lives, such as domestic violence. They offer all services at no cost to the women, thanks to the help of generous supporters.

"The founders of our Religious Community were convinced the world could be changed by educating women, and we want to continue to do that," explained Sister Cathy Feeney, the center's executive director.

Life is packed with potential for hope-filled change. Sometimes we're called to help make it happen.

He raises up the poor from the dust; He lifts the needy from the ash heap, to make them sit with princes and inherit a seat of honor. (1 Samuel 2:8)

Teach me Your ways, Lord, that I may serve others.

Making Sense of Suffering

Melanie Thernstrom had chronic pain. So she decided to write about it—and the suffering of others.

The Pain Chronicles blends cutting-edge research, cultural studies and medical history, with real people's stories in order to try to better understand pain. Here's some of what Thernstrom learned:

- Aging causes the brain to atrophy at a rate of a half a percent a year, but chronic pain causes it to do so twice as fast.

- Chronic pain is more common in women, as they generally have a lower pain tolerance.

- The brain can actually turn off pain. Continued studies of the brain's pain modulating system can perhaps help us train people to activate that "shut-off" switch themselves.

When we experience suffering in body or spirit, we should remember the Lord's invitation to come and rest in Him.

Come to Me, all you that are weary and are carrying heavy burdens, and I will give you rest. (Matthew 11:28)

Lord, I have faith in You; heal and guide me.

A Faithful Exchange

How often do you hear of a currency trader relinquishing his lucrative career in favor of monastic life? Former Wall Street trader Harry Quinson made that choice without hesitation, and gave all his money to charity. "I thought the spiritual part of my human life was more important than a career or making money," Quinson told *Fresh Air's* Terry Gross on National Public Radio.

For six years Harry resided in France's Tamie Abbey which housed an order of Trappist monks. After this prayerful epoch in his life, he transferred to a predominantly Muslim neighborhood where he teaches immigrant children, and works as a freelance translator. In 2009, he even served as monastic advisor for *Of Gods and Men*, a movie based on the real-life courageous actions of French monks in Algeria, some of whom Quinson knew.

Take after Quinson's example. Place less emphasis on money and more on the faithful exchange between yourself and the Lord. You'll be surprised at the bountiful profits you will reap.

In the house of the righteous there is much treasure. (Proverbs 15:6)

Lord, help us to make a rich investment of time and prayer into our spiritual lives.

Women on the Job

Most Americans are used to women working outside the home. In fact, women hold more than half of the labor force's professional and managerial jobs, according to the *AARP Bulletin*. Yet they still earn just 80 cents for every dollar a man earns.

Interestingly, women now receive 58 percent of all college degrees compared with men at 42 percent. They also earn 49 percent of medical degrees and 34 percent of theological degrees.

Long before these advances were made, there were the trailblazers. In 1849, Elizabeth Blackwell was the first American woman to earn a medical degree. Belva Ann Lockwood was the first woman to practice law before the U.S. Supreme Court in 1879. And in 2008, Ann Dunwoody became the first female four-star general.

The history of women has achievements to be celebrated—and more work to be done.

When they met her, they all blessed her with one accord and said..."You are the great pride of our nation." (Judith 15:9)

Thank You, Blessed Trinity, for all women and men who have gone before us seeking the good of others.

Singing America's Songs

With so many voices in America, musicians need to ensure that the songs of regular folks get heard.

Teacher and musician Betty Lomax Hawes, who died at age 88, carried on the folklore tradition. A *New York Times* obituary acknowledged her involvement with the Smithsonian Institution's Festival of American Folklife and the National Endowment for the Arts. The daughter of a song collector, Hawes performed with such folk singers as Woody Guthrie, Pete Seeger, and Baldwin "Butch" Hawes, her husband.

As a teenager she helped transcribe field recordings for her family's book, *Our Singing Country,* once entering Louisiana's notorious Angola state penitentiary to transcribe an inmate's song.

Today, an award in her honor ensures that others will carry on her work and that the voices of everyday people will be heard.

Value and enjoy the simple things in life, like a song.

Shout aloud and sing for joy, O royal Zion, for great in your midst is the Holy One of Israel. (Isaiah 12:6)

Jesus, may I raise my voice in song and prayer to praise You.

Called to Action

Nonna Bullock worked hard to become a nurse. After 15 years waitressing in a diner, she earned her GED and enrolled in nursing school at the University of Southern Mississippi.

Bullock was living 140 miles from New Orleans when Hurricane Katrina hit. "My nurse's hands itched to get there and help," she says.

But the danger and distance daunted her. As the months passed, Bullock wondered what to do. "Health care in New Orleans remained dire," she remembers. "Six hospitals were shut, and others coped with skeleton crews."

Then Bullock got a phone call from a nursing school friend who was working at Tulane Medical Center, in downtown New Orleans. That connection was just the link Bullock needed. She now divides her work between Tulane and her hometown.

It takes courage to help those in need. Doing so, however, can offer a renewed sense of purpose.

Be strong and bold; have no fear or dread of them, because it is the Lord your God who goes with you; He will not fail you or forsake you. (Deuteronomy 31:6)

Reveal to me my true calling, Spirit of Counsel.

Kindness, A Value To Cherish

Don't underestimate the value of so-called "small" gestures of kindness. Your thoughtful actions do make a difference.

When *Woman's World* magazine challenged readers to submit stories of everyday kindness, one mother wrote of how someone's generosity impressed her child.

"My 10-year-old son was flying his new kite on the beach—only to watch it crash and shatter into pieces," she wrote. The mother was heartbroken by the sadness on his face. But then both were uplifted when a nearby successful kite flyer handed the boy his spool of string.

"Take mine," he said. "I've had this kite since I was a kid, and I want it to go to someone who will have as much fun with it as I did."

The 10-year-old beamed and told his mother that one day he'd pass along this act of kindness to another child.

Kindness. Pass it on.

Those who withhold kindness from a friend forsake the fear of the Almighty. (Job 6:14)

Inspire us, Holy Spirit, to be kind with one another.

Stories Behind The Chinese Menu

In her book, *The Fortune Cookie Chronicles*, writer Jennifer 8. Lee, who calls herself an "American-born Chinese," talks about the facts and fiction of food history.

Chinese food's popularity (at least as prepared here) makes it almost as American as apple pie, with twice as many Chinese restaurants as there are McDonald's franchises.

Initially, Chinese people found barriers to their becoming U.S. citizens, starting with their arrival in California during the Gold Rush. They were also blocked from jobs in agriculture, mining and manufacturing. So they opened laundries and restaurants.

"Cleaning and cooking were both women's work," notes Lee. "They were not threatening to white laborers."

People of virtually every nation on earth have come to the United States of America and contributed to its success. That's still true today. Appreciate your heritage—and welcome new immigrants, new neighbors.

You shall not oppress a resident alien; you know the heart of an alien, for you were aliens in the land of Egypt. (Exodus 23:9)

Merciful Creator, remind us of our nation's past.

Versatile Salt

Salt is both valuable and intriguing, with many uses and a reputation both bad and good. Too much salt can be unhealthy. Yet it's also associated with good luck.

Lying nearly 1,200 feet below the city of Detroit is a century-old salt mine which is still producing. Man and machines extract salt from the mine walls. After processing it's sold to local governments for snow removal.

Salt has had many other uses throughout history besides seasoning, preserving food and melting snow. Thousands of years ago, it was used by Egyptians in burials. Salt has long been used by Jews in housewarmings, by Catholics in baptisms and by Hindus in weddings. And Mohammed said, "God sent down four blessings from the sky. Fire, water, iron and salt."

Certainly, the importance of this substance — or any other resource on Earth — should never be taken with a grain of salt.

Salt is good; but if salt has lost its taste, how can its saltiness be restored? (Luke 14:34)

Thank You for the variety of Your gifts on this magnificent planet of ours, Blessed Trinity.

Shifting Sands

Competitions abound from January to December, in every corner of the globe, to see who is the world's best sculptor—of sand.

A few people, like Lucinda "Sandy Feet" Wierenga, make a living out of building sand castles and other elaborate designs on the beach. Wierenga also gives private lessons on the art.

Most people, though, are amateurs who just enjoy the challenge.

For instance, one community in Oregon came together on a beach to create a dragon in the sand.

Although the tides wash away their accomplishments, these artists proceed undaunted. Said one, "It doesn't matter. The fun is in the creating."

Each day we should soak in all the beauty that surrounds us, ever grateful to God for those glimpses before they vanish.

Ever since the creation of the world His eternal power and divine nature, invisible though they are, have been understood and seen through the things He has made. (Romans 1:20)

Through life's changes, remain with me, Christ, my Savior.

Just Work

The rights of the American worker were won after long battles fought by bold, courageous activists throughout our history. That's why lunch breaks, overtime pay, and minimum wage requirements became part of labor and employment law.

But, according to a recent study by a group of economic justice organizations, these hard-won regulations still don't protect a significant number of the nation's low-wage workers.

A high percentage were denied a meal break or paid below the minimum wage, according to a study of individuals in food service, retail, construction and domestic jobs. The study's authors believe tougher enforcement of labor laws is vital.

Justice in the workplace should always be a two-way street: employers must put workers first and employees need to give a full measure for their daily wages.

Listen! The wages of the laborers who mowed your fields, which you kept back by fraud, cry out, and the cries of the harvesters have reached the ears of the Lord of hosts. (James 5:4)

We are Your instruments, Spirit of Justice. Use us to bring Your love to the world.

Paying Attention

Providing new students extra support is likely to pay dividends. The University of Cincinnati and other institutions of higher learning are finding creative ways to keep first-generation college students in school since so many do not make it without additional attention.

"Nationally, 89 percent of low-income first-generations leave college within six years without a degree," according to *USA Today*. "More than a quarter leave after their first year—four times the dropout rate of higher-income second-generation students."

New policies provide undergrads with access to tutors and mentors, a special study-skills class and peer support at their own off-campus residence. They also get wake-up calls, text messages or personal visits if they don't show up for class or have other problems.

Higher education is worth our extra investment in the lives of those at the greatest risk of failing.

God our Savior...desires everyone to be saved and to come to the knowledge of the truth. (1 Timothy 2:4)

Divine Teacher, help me to learn that my brothers and sisters of all ages deserve my attention and assistance.

What a Difference a "Thank You" Makes

Just as the Lord loves hearing our prayers of thanksgiving, so do people appreciate acknowledgement of their hard work.

Maureen Pratt, author of *Beyond Pain: Job, Jesus and Joy,* discovered the true power of giving thanks when she stopped to commend a man on his beautiful garden.

"His face took on a peculiar look," Pratt observed. "After a few moments of silence he said, 'I appreciate your saying that. Just before you came up to me, I'd decided to just sell the place and let them tear it down…After what you said, I think I'm going to keep the house and the garden as it is.' "

The man added that someone had been taking his flowers as soon as they bloomed. This selfishness had discouraged him, but Pratt's thanks had given him newfound courage to persevere.

One simple "thank you" can go a long way. Give thanks to the people who make a positive difference in your life.

For everything created by God is good, and nothing is to be rejected, provided it is received with thanksgiving; for it is sanctified by God's word and by prayer. (1 Timothy 4:4-5)

God, may we give thanks for all that is good and beautiful in our lives.

A Reason to Hope

Zachary was born with a chromosomal disorder causing him challenging physical and developmental impairments. He had trouble connecting with other kids.

Fortunately, Zachary found comfort in the stories of Brandy and Val, two shelter dogs who had been abused and abandoned but ultimately triumphed over adversity.

Ilene Fine, a friend of Zachary's parents, adopted and nursed the dogs back to health. She created a picture book for Zachary featuring the dogs' adventures and how they were healed. The ailing boy lived too far away to meet them but loved them through their stories.

The tales were so inspirational that Fine was encouraged to publish them. The *Brandy and Val* books have helped youngsters cope with various struggles.

"I'm so grateful we gave these dogs a second chance," notes Fine. "Brandy and Val took the love we gave them and are giving it back to these kids in a message of hope."

Blessed be...the God of all consolation, who consoles us in all our affliction.
(2 Corinthians 3:4)

Father, may we offer the discouraged reasons to hope.

Strive for Excellence

Writing in *Guideposts* magazine, Jon Gordon makes a case for the importance of setting excellence as our goal in life.

"Success is often measured by comparison to others. Excellence, on the other hand, is all about being the best we can be and maximizing our gifts, talents and abilities to perform at our highest potential."

According to Gordon, "We live in a world that loves to focus on success and loves to compare…[But] we must focus on being the best we can be and realize that our greatest competition is not someone else but ourselves."

Gordon contends that some of the most successful figures in athletics and business go on a quest for excellence. "Ironically," he writes, "when our goal is excellence, the outcome and byproduct is often success."

Discover your God-given talents and then develop them to the best of your ability.

Happy are those who find wisdom, and those who get understanding, for her income is better than silver, and her revenue better than gold. (Proverbs 3:18)

Help us, Lord, to strive for excellence to the benefit of ourselves and our world.

Woman on the Street

How can I make your life better?

That's the question Uyladia Jarmon-Colley asks young people she finds living on the streets of Atlanta, Georgia. A volunteer with a program geared to help homeless youth, she finds the answers are always different—from a healthy meal to a safe place to sleep. "We meet their immediate needs first, but ultimately our goal is get them off the streets," she says.

The mother of a toddler, Jarmon-Colley was laid off and looking for something positive to do while she hunted for a job. Her friend told her about the outreach program. "It helps me realize that I'm much better off than I thought," she observes. "These days I count my blessings."

Life is filled with challenges, great and small. While confronting our own, we can also keep an eye out for others in need.

Whoever pursues righteousness and kindness will find life and honor. (Proverbs 21:21)

Guard and guide me, Loving Master. Keep me safe from physical or spiritual harm.

Mychal's Message

When Father Mychal Judge was killed by falling debris during the 9/11 terrorist attacks in New York City, 11-year-old Shannon Hickey felt devastated. Father Mychal had been a close family friend throughout her life.

Shannon decided to honor the fallen priest's memory by collecting socks for the homeless who came to the bread line at St. Francis of Assisi Church, where he had lived. She also planned to give them Father Mychal's prayer: "Lord, take me where You want me to go / Let me meet who You want me to meet / Tell me what You want me to say / And keep me out of Your way."

After word spread, Shannon collected 1,500 pairs of socks. A new ministry called "Mychal's Message" was born. Since 2002, it has served the needy in New York and Pennsylvania by collecting and distributing over 200,000 new items to homeless and disadvantaged children and adults.

The Christophers honored Shannon with our 2011 James Keller Award (named after our founder) for showing what a young person with initiative and the gospel message can accomplish.

What great things can you accomplish?

Serve one another. (1 Peter 4:10)

Help us be people of love and action, Lord.

Dialogue to Better Understanding

"We want to begin by focusing on what we have in common, and at the same time identify the differences, and then try to identify points of further discussion," says Terrance Nichols, a professor at the University of St. Thomas in Minnesota.

Nichols and his Turkish-Muslim colleague, Adil Ozdemir, started the Muslim-Christian Dialogue Center to promote interfaith dialogue and better understanding. "You have to be who you are in a dialogue," Nichols said. "If you try to boil everything down to the lowest common denominator, you don't have a dialogue. You don't have anything to talk about."

Ozdemir says, "There is only one God and that is the God of all—the God of Abraham and Moses, and Jesus and Mohammed. No community can monopolize God, but we are all to compete, gently, to serve God who stands for peace and justice."

Those who say, "I love God," and hate their brothers and sisters, are liars; for those who do not love a brother or sister whom they have seen, cannot love God whom they have not seen. (1 John 4:20)

Open my mind to respect people of other beliefs, Lord.

A Knock at the Door — Twice

Father Tom Iwanowski recalls the horror of September 11, 2001. But he also remembers the contrasting hope he felt five years later on that same day.

Pastor of Our Lady of Czestochowa church in Jersey City, New Jersey at the time of the attack on the World Trade Center, the priest welcomed a woman who had been transported to safety by ferry along with hundreds of others. She came to the parish, just four blocks from the waterfront, and asked to use the phone to contact her family.

In 2006, on the fifth anniversary of the terrorist attack, the same woman returned, knocking again on the parish's rectory door. This time, she came to say, "Thanks."

"You never know how a small act of goodness will ripple through the lives of others," Father Iwanowski said.

Today, if anyone knocks at your heart's door looking for kindness, let them in!

If we are questioned today because of a good deed done to someone who was sick and are asked how this man has been healed, let it be known...that this man is standing before you in good health by the name of Jesus Christ. (Acts 4:9-10)

Lord, let me be Your compassion for those in need.

Embracing the Restless Soul

Do you often find yourself constantly asking that unanswerable question, "What's next, Lord?" Take comfort, you're not alone.

According to Steven Givens, author of *Embraced by God: Facing Chemotherapy with Faith*, such feelings are not only natural but in the long run help us to become better Christians.

"God made us to be restless," Givens writes. "He knew this restlessness would push us ever toward him. God knew that, with the help of the Spirit, we wouldn't stop, wouldn't accept the easy way of skimming by on the bare minimum of spiritual living."

Just like any worthwhile blessing in life—whether this blessing is a good education, a decent job or the person with whom you wish to spend your life—religious maturity is something that must be continuously worked on if it has any chance of surviving. The initial labor might be difficult, but the end result will make it all worthwhile.

God is our refuge and strength, a very present help in trouble. Therefore, we will not fear. (Psalm 46:1-2)

Heavenly Father, may we learn to embrace our restlessness as a means of bringing us closer to You.

Folding Lessons

Annie had a day filled with household chores, among them, seemingly endless laundry. She was weary. With all she had to do, Annie also had her four-year-old grandson, Sam, for the day and he was determined to help with everything.

The two stood in their neighborhood laundromat, loading and emptying washing machines, and then dryers. Sam pulled clothes from both machines, showing his grandmother his "big muscles." Watching him squeeze out a tiny muscle made Annie smile.

Sam did the folding, too, and in the process, Annie's towels ended up rolled into balls. Usually particular about her laundry, this day Annie decided to leave the towels that way. When she would use them, she thought, she'd remember a fun afternoon, despite all the work.

In our own lives, there are times when it's less important to do the perfect job than it is to enjoy the best of times.

Has anyone planted a vineyard but not yet enjoyed its fruit? He should go back to his house, or he might die in the battle, and another be first to enjoy its fruit.
(Deuteronomy 20:6)

Paraclete, bless my work this day with joy and gratitude.

Bouncing Back after Setbacks

Despite a long series of health problems, Dawn Forgione is able to face life with an upbeat attitude.

"I love to be a positive role model and show others that a diagnosis is not a death sentence," she says.

This middle-aged mother of two 20-something daughters cultivates an optimistic attitude. Her hopeful spirit has helped her deal with various cancers, knee and hip surgeries and other health challenges. She cares for herself with medical checkups, regular exercise, and a healthy diet.

And Forgione helps others through such groups as the American Cancer Society and the Children's Cancer Care Center in Miami, Florida.

Some people seem blessed with sunny personalities. Others have learned how to make the best of things. Some ideas: cultivate a spirit of gratitude; take good care of yourself; help others.

They are to do good, to be rich in good works, generous, and ready to share, thus storing up for themselves the treasure of a good foundation for the future, so that they may take hold of the life that really is life.
(1 Timothy 6:18-19)

Jesus, nourish and heal us.

Highway Safety

It was welcome news to learn that America's traffic fatalities have hit a 60-year low.

According to a story in the *Washington Post*, highway deaths have plunged because of improved street and vehicle designs as well as resolute campaigns against driving drunk or distracted.

The information was obtained from a 2010 report by the National Highway Traffic Safety Administration based on statistics from each state.

The *Post* quotes Barbara Harsha, executive director of the Governors Highway Safety Association, citing such important factors as "increased seat belt use, stronger enforcement of drunk-driving laws, better roads, safer vehicles and an increasingly well-coordinated approach to safety among state stakeholders and the federal government."

Individuals and families obviously have a huge stake in the matter also. So save texting, talking, make-up application and so on for a safer time and place.

Those who listen to me will be secure and will live at ease, without dread of disaster. (Proverbs 1:33)

Infuse us with a concern for safety, Holy Spirit.

Being a Mercy Volunteer

Inspired by her brother's volunteer work in East Africa and her own service efforts at the College of St. Benedict, Maria Conroy from Monticello, Minnesota, decided to do something different after graduation.

She contacted Mercy Volunteer Corps about working at Mercy Center, which serves immigrants in the Mott Haven section of the Bronx, New York. Mott Haven is the poorest congressional district in the U.S.

Conroy ran the kindergarten-to-second-grade after-school program, providing both literacy and arts-based education to the kids. She told *Christopher Closeup* host Tony Rossi that her volunteering has turned into a determination to earn a degree in social work so helping others can become a lifelong path.

She concluded, "Humanity can do a lot to hurt each other and to bring each other down. But when we unite and love each other and...do what I think God has created and willed us to do (which) is live in union and live in love, there's nothing more powerful than that."

You shall love the Lord your God with all your heart, and with all your soul, and with all your strength...and love your neighbor as yourself. (Luke 10:27)

Help us become united in love for You, Father.

Joyful Stories Born of Struggle

You are probably familiar with the children's book character Curious George, the mischievous monkey. Since its publication in 1941, the series has sold 27 million copies in more than a dozen languages.

The husband-and-wife author team, Margret and H. A. Rey, began penning the stories in the late 1930s in Germany. Both Jewish, the Reys had a narrow escape after a grueling and frightening journey through several countries—made on bicycle and on foot—to get away from the Nazis in 1940.

The vivid colors that serve as a trademark of the *Curious George* series were deliberately used by the authors, who wanted to create art that was joyful, fun and an antidote to the dismal gloom of wartime Europe.

Optimism and faith can enable us to overcome the worst of circumstances. Never stop hoping for a better day ahead.

Then the man said, "You shall no longer be called Jacob, but Israel, for you have striven with God and with humans, and have prevailed." (Genesis 32:28)

Renew our faith, Loving God.

Coming Home to Roost

If you're a parent with an adult child living at home, you are not alone. The Pew Research Center reports that roughly 20 million people age 18 to 34 live with their parents, representing about 30 percent of that age group.

Many of these younger adults have resorted to "coming home to mom and dad" because of a stagnant economy and dismal employment opportunities. Whatever the cause, the arrangement can lead to disagreements and tension if not handled well.

Experts agree that establishing guidelines is critical to harmony in this situation. For example:

- Set a time limit to the arrangement.
- Keep communication open and frequent.
- Give each other space and respect.

Make sure adult children share in expenses, chores and other responsibilities.

Honor your father and your mother, so that your days may be long in the land that the Lord your God is giving you. (Exodus 20:12)

Guide us in our relationships, Christ Jesus.

Canine Counselors?

Each week, 17-year-old Melanie Adelman and her mom attend an after-school reading program for high-risk students.

Instead of having trouble focusing on reading as she does in the classroom, here Melanie is relaxed and ready to learn. The difference? Stetson, an 8-year-old toy poodle, sits at her side.

Therapy dogs, as they're called, are simply household pets that are registered or certified through a therapy-related organization to bring positive energy and stress relief to kids like Melanie. Good tempered and obedient, these dogs provide soothing and relaxing care to kids in schools, hospitals, libraries and other facilities that tend to kids in need.

What's more, even the dog volunteer gains benefits from such work. Experts say exposure to new faces and surroundings can help keep dogs active and healthier.

It seems the wonders of God's creations never cease!

Your righteousness is like the mighty mountains, Your judgments are like the great deep; You save humans and animals alike, O Lord. (Psalm 36:6)

Protect helpless animals from neglect and abuse, Son of God.

Believing and Basketball

Throughout the basketball season, high school student Jason McElwain would remind basketball coach Jim Johnson that he had promised him a few minutes of playing time.

McElwain, who is autistic, had tried out for the team at New York's Greece Athena High School three years in a row. Not selected, he agreed instead to be team manager. Then came the night he got those few minutes—about three to be exact—and scored 20 points. The key to McElwain's success, according to his coach: total perseverance to reach his dream.

In his book, *A Coach and a Miracle: Life Lessons from a Man who Believed in an Autistic Boy,* Johnson invites readers to set their own self-improvement goals, and to focus on serving others. His work features reactions from families who have struggled with disabilities and acceptance.

Having faith in God and ourselves while also believing in others form a great game plan for life.

There are varieties of services, but the same Lord. (1 Corinthians 12:5)

Lord, bless all I do this day.

Setting Your Priorities

What are your priorities?

Dr. Stephen R. Covey tells this story which he found to be an unforgettable illustration of setting priorities. A speaker used a concrete demonstration to make a point to some high-powered business students. He set out a one-gallon, wide-mouthed jar and filled it to the top with about 12 fist-sized rocks.

The students all agreed the jar was full. But then he was able to pour in gravel and shake the jar. He again asked if it was full. Now the class wasn't as sure. Then the speaker dumped in sand which filled in even smaller spaces. Finally, he poured in water from a pitcher.

"The truth this illustration teaches us is: If you don't put the big rocks in first, you'll never get them in at all."

Decide what the most important things in your life are—and then make room for them.

Take care that you do not forget the Lord your God, by failing to keep His commandments. (Deuteronomy 8:11)

Blessed Trinity, keep me from being overwhelmed by life's little problems so that I can concentrate on what really matters.

Being First

Every city is proud of the accomplishments of its people. Pittsburgh is no exception. Here are some of Pittsburgh's "firsts:"

The city was the location of the first heart-liver-kidney transplant in 1989. The first internet emoticon, a "smiley," was created in 1980 by a Carnegie Mellon University scientist.

The first "Mr. Yuk" sticker was created in 1971 at the Poison Center at Children's Hospital after research showed that the skull and crossbones generally used to identify poisons meant nothing to children. In that same year, the city hosted the first night World Series baseball game.

In 1967, folks ate the first Big Macs there. In 1954 came the first U.S. public TV station (WQED). And the first polio vaccine was developed by Dr. Jonas Salk at the University of Pittsburgh in 1953.

If you want to be first, make it something of which you will be proud.

"I am the Alpha and the Omega," says the Lord God, "who is and who was and who is to come." (Revelation 1:8)

You are the Alpha and the Omega, the Beginning and the End, Holy God. May I desire Your will above all things.

Youngsters Respond To Challenge

Sister Jane Meyer, a Texas high-school principal, used a unique way to challenge students to raise money for Haitian earthquake relief. The 71-year-old educator told the youngsters if they raised $25,000 by Ash Wednesday, she would jump out of a plane, notes a story in *The Week*.

How far would these kids go to see their principal, a Dominican nun for more than 50 years, take a 14,000-foot skydiving leap?

The students staged talent shows, and they held bake sales and raffles. According to the story, they "blew past their goal, raising more than $88,000."

The effort was for a good cause and serious business. But it was also fun for the students to see their principal practicing what she preached.

"I always tell our students they have to take good risks and stretch themselves," said Sister Jane Meyer, once again safely planted on terra firma.

Do not, therefore, abandon that confidence of yours; it brings a great reward. For you need endurance, so that when you have done the will of God, you may receive what was promised. (Hebrews 10:35-36)

Dear God, encourage us to take important risks.

The Human Experience

The powerful documentary *The Human Experience* earned a Christopher Award in 2011. It profiled brothers Jeffrey and Clifford Azize, who set out on a trek around the world with their friends to discover the essence of the human spirit.

They lived with the homeless on the streets of New York, cared for disabled children in Peru, and visited victims of leprosy and AIDS in Africa.

Along the way, they explored questions about the purpose of life and the inherent dignity of every person.

Their journey reminds us that even society's outcasts aren't as different from us as we may think. As one of the lepers in Africa states, "We all are the same. You are my brother. That's why you need to love everybody."

Each person is precious in the eyes of God. Let's remember to treat each other with the love and respect God demands.

Pursue peace with everyone, and the holiness without which no one will see the Lord. (Hebrews 12:14)

May our lives testify that everyone is created in Your image and likeness, Lord.

Sleep Out

It's said that you can never judge people until you walk a mile in their shoes. What if this adage applied to sleeping in someone else's bed or, as in the case of a homeless man or woman, cardboard box?

For the past three years, over 200 students from St. Raphael Academy and four other Catholic schools in the Providence, Rhode Island Diocese, have gathered at the Cathedral of SS. Peter and Paul to experience a touch of homelessness themselves.

According to Katherine Dancause, writing in the *Rhode Island Catholic Correspondent,* her home state had the highest levels of homelessness in 2008. One night of sleeping outside in a flimsy cardboard box in below-zero weather encourages pupils to empathize with the plight of the impoverished. No student walks away without gaining a newfound understanding of homelessness.

God says the poor will always be with us. We should reach out and assist them in any way possible.

The righteous know the rights of the poor. (Proverbs 29:7)

Jesus, may we always remember to reach out to the impoverished.

Kosher Kitchen for the Needy

Many communities have food pantries, where basic staples such as bread, milk and canned food are provided for the hungry, impoverished or unemployed. But what happens to poor people who follow a restricted diet as part of their religious practices?

The Bnai Raphael Cheese Store and Food Pantry in the heavily Orthodox Jewish section of Brooklyn, New York, has answered the call. It provides certified kosher foods to needy families as well as to 36 kosher food programs in the state, enabling recipients to follow their dietary guidelines.

Goldie Greenberg, 66, appreciates the service, since her salary as a home attendant doesn't allow her to afford kosher foods. "This saves my life," she says.

The number of families registered for the Pantry's services jumped from 800 in 2007 to 1,500 in 2009.

Religious tolerance is a basic principle upon which our nation was built. Treat followers of all religions with respect.

Be at peace with one another. (Mark 9:50)

Steer us toward respecting the religious beliefs of others, Prince of Peace.

Six Ways of Restoring Balance

With today's busy lifestyles, it's no wonder people of all ages feel overwhelmed. According to Dr. Gregory Popcak, there are six ways of restoring much-needed balance in people's hectic lives:

1. Own your life. If the choices you've made have caused you to be overwhelmed, make better choices in the future.

2. Remember that time, energy, and willpower are limited resources.

3. Put relationships first. Studies show that people in strong relationships lead more stress-free lives.

4. Instill routines, rituals and rhythms.

5. Embrace "no." Know yourself and what you can and cannot do. You won't be the only one who benefits.

6. Refresh with short time-outs. Taking short time-outs can often help to refuel your drained brain.

God hates us to be overly anxious about our lives. Take each day as it comes and trust the Lord to take care of the rest.

Trust in the Lord, and do good. (Psalm 37:3)

Jesus, may we strive to instate greater balance in our lives.

Big Screen Lessons

Why not make tonight family movie night?

You might start with three films that form the core of a middle-school curriculum created by Martin Scorsese: *Mr. Smith Goes to Washington*, *To Kill a Mockingbird* and *The Day the Earth Stood Still*. George Lucas, Steven Spielberg and other filmmakers contributed to *The Story of Movies* project which introduces a new generation to the magic and lessons of movies.

These films "immediately grab interest and attention, and, by the end, have taught or reaffirmed some lessons about life that are worth knowing," said Robert Osborne, host of Turner Classic Movies.

All three share a distinctive style of visual storytelling and have children playing key roles. In addition, Spielberg noted, they feature "one person who can make a difference in all our lives, someone who is fighting on your behalf."

Enjoyment and inspiration. Good show.

When he came and saw the grace of God, he rejoiced, and he exhorted them all to remain faithful to the Lord with steadfast devotion. (Acts 11:23)

One person can change someone else's world. Encourage me to be that person today, Paraclete.

Saintly, Yes; Timid, No

Popular art has been guilty over the centuries of depicting angels as mild-mannered beings with gentle personas. Biblical authority tells otherwise, however.

Take St. Raphael, the Archangel. The patron saint of travelers, St. Raphael has been known to be a celestial guide and healer, filled with gentle tendencies. However, as told in the Book of Tobit, Raphael not only helped Tobit's son, Tobias, on his journey, but helped Tobias find a wife, expelled a demon, and cured his father, Tobit, of blindness.

It seems popular culture got it wrong with St. Gabriel as well. Known as the angel sent by God to tell Mary she would bear a son called Jesus, Scripture also tells us Gabriel announced to Zechariah the coming birth of John the Baptist. He appears in the Old Testament as well, explaining the vision of the horned ram. He also prophesied the time before the coming of Christ.

Usually, it's important to get *all* the facts to know the truth.

For the Son of Man is to come with His angels in the glory of His Father. (Matthew 16:27)

May Your angels guide me toward truth, Lord.

Faith and Challenges

For young Christians in Nepal, living out their faith can be a daunting task. Most in the Asian country are Buddhist or Hindu; Christians are but a tiny minority.

"The last time I told my friends about my faith, they smiled and looked at me as if I were an alien," explained Mhendo Tamang, a member of Our Lady of the Assumption Catholic Church in Kathmandu, the capital city. Other young people share her isolation.

Local church leaders are reaching out to these youth, offering retreats and other ways for them to connect. Said one teen, "I liked the way we got together, prayed and shared ideas."

Facing life alone is challenging indeed. Not only do we long to share our sorrows and joys, but also our deepest beliefs. Reach out to comfort or celebrate with someone today.

Who will separate us from the love of Christ? Will hardship, or distress, or persecution, or famine, or nakedness, or peril, or sword? (Romans 8:35)

Separated from You I can do nothing; stay close, Holy Wisdom.

Responding to Rudeness with Love

One of the most beloved saints in modern times is St. Therese of Lisieux, also known as the "Little Flower." The reason she's so popular is that ordinary people can relate to her spirituality and even her struggles with faith.

Brother Joseph Schmidt wrote a comprehensive biography of the Little Flower called *Everything is Grace: The Life and Way of Therese of Lisieux.* While discussing the book on our *Christopher Closeup* radio show/podcast, he said that when Therese first entered the convent, the environment was very "dysfunctional" due to the nuns exhibiting a lot of harshness toward one another.

Instead of taking part in it, Therese acted patient, kind and loving with everyone, even when she was on the receiving end of some cruel remark. Due to her influence, the residents of the convent slowly became more loving toward one another.

St. Therese described her vocation simply as "love." It was a Christ-like love that changed many hearts and minds. It is a love we should emulate today.

If I speak in the tongues of mortals and of angels but have not love, I am a noisy gong. (1 Corinthians 13:1)

Jesus, help me respond to hatred with love.

Swinging for Charity

Ben Sater wasn't a typical 11-year-old. At an age when most kids are playing video games, he was organizing a charity golf tournament. Called KidSwing, it supports a Dallas hospital that had performed two free surgeries on him. To everyone's surprise, he managed to bring in $20,000 at that first tournament.

Eight years later, KidSwing is a runaway success. It attracted 20 corporate sponsors this past year, donating goods and funds to the cause. Nearly $1 million has been raised.

To make a difference, we need only have a goal in mind and the determination to see it fulfilled. There's no excuse for complacency. Don't fool yourself into thinking there's nothing you can do. Go out and do your part to change things for the better.

Consider how to provoke one another to love and good deeds...encouraging one another. (Hebrews 10:24-25)

God, please grant me the courage to go out and act as an agent for change in the world.

Whispers in the Train Station

There's a spot in New York City's Grand Central Station, right near the famous Oyster Bar, where a whisper can sound like a shout to someone at a distance.

In fact, a person facing one corner of the large arched entryway can be heard—loud and clear—by another facing the opposite corner. According to experts, this happens because the whisperer's voice follows the curve of the domed ceiling.

Scientific explanations aside, the location is a popular one for tourists—and for marriage proposals!

In prayer, we can present the whispered longings of our heart, confident that God hears our every word.

Regard Your servant's prayer and his plea, O Lord my God, heeding the cry and the prayer that Your servant prays to You...May You hear from heaven Your dwelling place: hear and forgive. (2 Chronicles 6:19,21)

Loving Lord, above all, I listen for Your voice, ready to do Your will.

A Prayer For Marriage

Today we'd like to share a Christopher prayer for Husbands and Wives:

Lord, inspire those men and women who bear the titles "husband" and "wife."

Help them to look to You, to themselves, and to one another to rediscover the fullness and mystery they once felt in their union.

Let them be honest enough to ask "Where have we been together and where are we going?"

Let them be brave enough to question, "How have we failed?"

Let them each be foolhardy enough to say, "For me, *we* come first."

Help them together to believe how fragile, yet how powerful—how weak yet how strong—how impossible yet attainable their love can be.

Give "Husband" and "Wife" the courage to be for each other a person rather than a title. Amen.

Therefore a man leaves his father and his mother and clings to his wife, and they become one flesh. (Genesis 2:24)

Father, let Your love and light guide husbands and wives.

Perfectly Miserable

The *Gospel Herald* newspaper offered these tips to show how you can make yourself "perfectly miserable."

Start by talking about yourself constantly; then, listen greedily to what others say about you; expect to be appreciated whenever you do something; act suspicious, jealous and envious around others; never forgive a criticism, and never forget a service you have rendered; shirk your duties if you can; do as little as possible for others; and last but not least, love yourself supremely.

If we constantly focus on ourselves, we will never find happiness. On the other hand, if we never think about ourselves and our needs, we'll also be miserable.

The trick is to find a balance. So think of others without neglecting yourself.

You show me the path of life. In Your presence there is fullness of joy; in Your right hand are pleasures forevermore. (Psalm 16:11)

Jesus, help me avoid selfishness so I can respond mercifully and compassionately to the needs of others.

Cube of Love

The sayings on the sides of the colorful square box appeal to the better part of human nature. The phrases encourage all to "love everyone," to "share the other's hurt or joy," and to "love your enemy."

The Cube of Love was created by Chiara Lubitch, founder of the Catholic Church's Focolare Movement. Used with schoolchildren in some 180 countries, it's a positive response to bullying issues, as well as a road map for good behavior.

"We roll it each morning and talk about the point that comes up," offered Angela Di Prospero, a teacher in Canada. "It just takes a few minutes to reflect, then one good thing leads to another."

Choices surround us. In prayer, we can always find a way to reflect our love for God and neighbor.

> **The Spirit of the Lord is upon me, because He has anointed me to bring good news to the poor. He has sent me to proclaim release to the captives...to let the oppressed go free, to proclaim the year of the Lord's favor.**
> **(Luke 4:18-19)**

Bless me, Lord, with a share of Your wisdom.

Sharing Experiences to Give Hope

Madonna School in Omaha, Nebraska, is a Catholic institution that educates children with special needs. The school's president, Jay Dunlap, recognized that parents of the students at his school have a unique insight into raising children with physical disabilities, Down syndrome, developmental delays, autism and Asperger syndrome.

With this in mind, Dunlap and the parents formed a helpline that offers advice and understanding to parents of children with special needs.

The idea of the helpline came about when Dunlap saw research that showed many people choose abortion when they discover their child will have Down syndrome. Jay decided that the parents at Madonna School would be a great resource to offer direction for parents in crisis.

Sharing your life experiences with others can give them hope to continue their journey. Look for opportunities within your community, friends and family to provide support and a listening ear.

**I will strengthen you, I will help you.
(Isaiah 41:10)**

Lord, I ask two things of You today: Tell me what You want me to do, and give me the courage to do it.

Being a Christ-bearer

Father James Keller, the founder of The Christophers, once wrote these words about the mission of the Christopher movement:

"Each of us has, by the grace of God, the power to change the world for the better. Every act of care and concern for others has a ripple effect, touching many lives.

"So go into the marketplace—into a job of your own choosing—without fanfare or flag-waving. Where there is hate, bring in love; where there is darkness, carry light.

"The mere fact that you are alive—no matter your age, the state of your health or your physical condition—means that you have been chosen by God to perform some work that no other person can do.

"Each of us is an instrument of supernatural grace. We do not have to depend on our own limited ability, but have the whole of heaven behind us, even when we seem to fail."

What actions can you take in order to be a Christopher—a Christ-bearer—today?

We know that all things work together for good for those who love God, who are called according to His purpose. (Romans 9:8)

Lead me toward my divine purpose, Father.

Facing Death — Together

What do you say to a dying friend or family member? Should we even speak about what he or she is facing?

According to Donna Authers, professional caregiver and author of *A Sacred Walk,* talking about what's going on can actually be a very healthy thing to do.

"Most people at the end of their lives have unspoken fears, concerns about the things they should've done, what they didn't finish," she says, "and they would really love to have someone they can tell these things to."

Authers also advocates just listening to whatever memories or topics come up, and making it easy for the dying person to see and talk with loved ones as much as possible.

Difficult times are best endured with the help of others, just as sharing good times magnifies the joy.

Two are better than one, because they have a good reward for their toil. For if they fall, one will lift up the other. (Ecclesiastes 4:9-10)

I put my faith in You, Lord. Embrace my suffering and end my pain.

Engaging Young Minds

Education can be out of this world.

"The Mars Student Imaging Program is certainly one of the greatest educational programs developed," said teacher Dennis Mitchell. His seventh-grade science class at a Cottonwood, California, middle school participates in a research project studying images of the Red Planet taken by a NASA spacecraft.

The program "gives the students a good understanding of the way research is conducted and how that research can be important for the scientific community," said Mitchell.

The students were able to commission a Mars-orbiting camera and discovered what appeared to be a Martian skylight—a hole in the roof of a cave on Mars. Surprisingly, this pit crater "is certainly new to us," said a U.S. Geological Survey scientist, and is only the second found in that area of the Red Planet.

Curiosity and imagination can lead us to wonderful new places.

The human mind plans the way, but the Lord directs the steps. (Proverbs 16:9)

Divine Creator, help us to use all the talents and abilities with which You have blessed us.

A Gringo in the Fields

Writer Gabriel Thompson was fascinated by the lettuce industry in Arizona, especially in view of the immigration debate. He says that migrant workers who support the industry are in short supply, largely due to an aging workforce, immigration crackdowns and border delays that discourage workers with green cards from commuting to the fields from their homes in Mexico.

Deciding to become a worker himself, Thompson learned the "five day rule," a maxim among seasoned field workers: "Survive the first five days and you'll be fine." An aching back and painfully sore muscles are all in a day's work.

In addition to grueling exertion, the work involves skillful hands. Cutting the lettuce from the trunk, then shaking and bagging it, requires agility, speed and concentration. In all, the writer experienced firsthand the sweat and toil these workers expend every day.

Pray for farm workers and all those who do tough jobs most of us reject.

You shall not oppress a resident alien. (Exodus 23:9)

Protect day laborers from exploitation, Father.

In God's Hands

Debra Tomaselli had every reason to be fearful. She had just received an e-mail that stated a gunman was loose in her Florida neighborhood. Strangely, Tomaselli felt more sympathy for the faceless gunman than for her own welfare.

"How fearful it must be to hide behind the barrel of a gun," Debra reflected in her syndicated column. "How alone and afraid, small and powerless he must feel."

As hard as Tomaselli tried to work that afternoon, her thoughts and prayers inevitably turned to this man, whom she learned was now being trapped in an apartment surrounded by SWAT teams. Abandoning work for the moment, Debra fell to her knees and succumbed to prayer— prayer for the gunman, prayer for the safety of others, prayer for an ultimately "peaceful resolution." The next morning, she discovered that the gunman "submitted peacefully."

If a problem or situation overwhelms you, never attempt to face it alone. Instead, leave it in God's hands. He alone has the power to convert troubled souls.

O Lord our God, save us. (2 Kings 19:19)

May we not falter in the face of danger or adversity but rather lift our struggles up to You, merciful and loving Father.

Taking a Walk

One Saturday morning, Maggie decided to catch up on all the errands she'd been putting off.

Once on the main avenue in her neighborhood, she immediately ran into a friend. The two discussed plants and their families for close to an hour.

Moving along, she met a local shop owner and his daughter, on their way to his store. The little girl begged Maggie to walk with them, telling her every detail of the past week.

Leaving them, she ran into two more friends, a husband and wife. He had been struggling with health issues, suffering another setback just the past week. As they talked, the couple suggested lunch; the morning was now gone.

Maggie decided to join them, realizing that a to-do list is not nearly as important as being there for those around us.

I pray that you may have the power to comprehend...and to know the love of Christ that surpasses knowledge, so that you may be filled with all the fullness of God.
(Ephesians 3:18-19)

Strengthen me with Your presence, Redeemer. Help me remember You are always near.

A Father's Lesson

In her column for the *St. Louis Post-Dispatch,* journalist Colleen Carroll Campbell wrote a remembrance of her father, Thomas Carroll Sr., when he lost his battle with Alzheimer's.

Diagnosed in 1996, Carroll became more and more dependent as the disease progressed. Yet the joy and compassion he possessed throughout his life never left him.

Colleen recalled, "Led into a room full of dementia patients, he would find his way to the corner where the most distressed one among them was muttering incoherently…He would whisper, 'We're all in God's hands,' and stroke her arm until she grew quiet and calm. 'I like to take care of people,' he would tell me."

Colleen concluded, "Alzheimer's eventually robbed my father of everything a disease can take from a man. But it could not steal his joy. Cultivated through a lifetime of putting people before possessions, principle before prestige, and love of God and family before his own desires, Dad's joy seemed to spring from some inexhaustible source—from a place the plaques and tangles of Alzheimer's could not reach."

Faith, hope and love abide. (1 Corinthians 13:13)

Savior, help us spread joy even in times of suffering.

Mailing a Tree

Each fall, Lisa Scherer's sister Cindy gathers 20 acorns that have fallen from the old oak tree in her backyard.

Then, she chooses 20 random people from the phone book, and mails each one an acorn, along with a note containing directions on how to plant the seed and information on the value of trees.

While the Pennsylvania woman realizes not all the acorns will get planted, Scherer says in a letter to *Guideposts* magazine that her sister hopes at least one of them ends up in someone's backyard or maybe in a community park: "She likes to believe that from the single oak tree in her backyard, she has continued its legacy and helped to honor one of God's mightiest creations."

All of us are partners with God in His creation, called to nurture and preserve all life around us.

Out of the ground the Lord God made to grow every tree that is pleasant to the sight and good for food. (Genesis 2:9)

Plant Your love within my heart, Lord, that I may share it with others.

Blessings and Responsibilities

Grammy Award-winning singer Amy Grant was taught by her grandparents that "with great blessing comes great responsibility." It's a lesson she continues to live out.

On the *Christopher Closeup* radio show/podcast, Amy remembered receiving a call from a friend who has a son with cerebral palsy and an overwhelming number of medical bills. This friend didn't ask Amy for the money. She just wanted ideas on how she could raise it.

Within two weeks, Amy and some colleagues pulled together a huge yard sale fundraiser in Nashville, Tennessee. They made $25,000 in one day.

Amy was thrilled by the joyful atmosphere at the yard sale. She said, "There were people from both sides of the tracks; every nationality from Nashville was there. I look at that and think, 'How boring if somebody had written a check for $25,000.' And how exciting when a few hundred people in a community came together. There was so much love in that yard, it was awesome!"

Bring the people in your community together to share your blessings with those in need.

**Let all that you do be done in love.
(1 Corinthians 16:14)**

Help us be models of compassion, Lord.

Connecting with God Through Work

Writing in the magazine *Lutheran Woman Today*, Greg Pierce had this to say about finding value in the work that you do:

"How would we act differently if we were convinced that what we do every day was a call from God? Would we see the meaning of what we do differently?

"Co-workers, clients, even fellow commuters can be seen as opportunities of grace rather than obstacles to be overcome.

"If we had a sense of vocation, we would balance the various responsibilities in our life—job, family, community and church. To think that there would be even one child of God who is not called to something important would be to underestimate God's concern for each of us."

Look at your work as a way to connect with God—and with your own human potential.

We have not ceased praying for you...so that you may lead lives worthy of the Lord, fully pleasing to Him, as you bear fruit in every good work and as you grow in the knowledge of God. (Colossians 1:9-10)

Help me approach my work in a spirit of cooperation with You, Divine Savior.

Healthy Guilt

When a medical student cheated on the first lab quiz of the year, her instructor caught her.

After class, the student sought out her teacher to say how ashamed she felt. The two discussed the pressures of medical school, along with the student's personal insecurities. The young woman resolved not to cheat again.

Therapist Joan Borysenko describes this as "healthy guilt." She says, "The process of responsibility, self-inquiry, and letting go of the past deepens self-respect. It's called forgiveness. Forgiveness creates a shift in perception that permits us to see our mistake as an opportunity to learn rather than as proof of how bad we are."

When you hurt others, own up to your mistake, make amends and determine to do better. Remember that even good people sometimes do bad things.

Then I acknowledged my sin to You, and I did not hide my iniquity; I said, "I will confess my transgressions to the Lord," and You forgave the guilt of my sin. (Psalm 32:5)

Your mercy cleanses me, Savior.

Communicating as Husband and Wife

The joy at the birth of Emmett and Mary's baby girl was soon followed by loud arguments.

With so much attention focused on the baby, Emmett felt that Mary no longer loved him. Mary was having a hard time balancing her roles as wife and mother. Each partner felt hurt, angry, and alone.

Their solution was to talk about their feelings. Mary told Emmett about her confusion over her new role as a mom; Emmett shared his insecurity about her love for him.

When they took the time to really understand each other, Emmett and Mary's problems became more manageable. And they agreed to take time to be a "couple" as well as a "family."

Remember to treat your spouse the way you want to be treated. A little consideration and understanding will go a long way.

(Make) your ear attentive to wisdom and...your heart to understanding...cry out for insight, and raise your voice for understanding...then you will...find the knowledge of God.
(Proverbs 2:1-5)

Help us to be honest and humble in discussing our problems, Father.

An Extra Leg Up

At age sixteen, Jordan Thomas lost both his legs below the knee when a wave knocked him into a boat propeller while he was scuba diving with his family.

Though he was eventually able to get prosthetic legs, Jordan was surprised to learn that many insurance companies don't cover the costs of prostheses for young people. In response, he established a foundation to pay for the artificial limbs of children whose families can't afford them.

To date, Thomas—now age 22 and a student at Rollins College in Winter Park, Florida—has raised almost $1 million toward the replacement of prosthetic limbs for five children until they turn eighteen.

"That may not seem like a lot, but kids outgrow prostheses, on average, every 18 months," he explained in *Parade* magazine. "It's an injustice that kids are denied prostheses. It's my responsibility to do as much as I can to help."

The Lord put us on this earth to help one another. He never wants us to feel alone in our sorrows. Oftentimes, it is in easing other people's sufferings that we ourselves are most comforted.

Build up each other. (1 Thessalonians 5:11)

Messiah, may we fill the emptiness in our lives with compassion toward others.

What Good Is Religion?

One day, a believer and a skeptic went for a walk. The skeptic said, "Look at the trouble and misery in the world after thousands of years of religion. What good is religion?"

His companion noticed a child, filthy with grime, playing in the gutter. The believer said, "We've had soap for generation after generation, yet look how dirty that child is. Of what value is soap?"

The skeptic protested, "But soap can't do anything unless it's used!"

"Exactly," replied the believer.

At the heart of most religions is a call to serve others. But that call has to be understood and put into action. This world will never improve if you just sit around and wish things were different.

You have to live your faith. Then you will be changing our world—and yourself—for the better.

Religion that is pure and undefiled before God, the Father, is this: to care for orphans and widows in their distress, and to keep oneself unstained by the world. (James 1:27)

Father, give us the wisdom and strength to love You and our neighbors.

Turning in His Business Suit

James Martin was a corporate executive with a closet full of expensive suits, a big salary, long hours and constant pressure.

Then he watched a documentary on the famed Trappist monk Thomas Merton, and asked his parish priest where he could go to become a holy person. The priest pointed to the Society of Jesus, the Jesuits.

"I went and got brochures on my lunch hour," he recalled. Initially, he ripped them up, but it was too late. He had a longing to connect with God and the rest of the world.

He left corporate life and became a priest. These days, Father Martin, author of the Christopher Award-winning book, *The Jesuit Guide to (Almost) Everything: A Spirituality for Real Life*, helps the doubtful and the devout make God the center of their lives.

As he writes in the book, "God is always inviting us to encounter the transcendent in the everyday; the key is noticing."

What's your life about? Helping others focus on God's love each day is a perfect purpose.

Strive first for the kingdom of God. (Matthew 6:33)

You know and love me, Gentle Jesus, and I have hope.

Struggling to Succeed

After becoming pregnant at a young age, Jocelyn Morales confronted the challenge of being a parent without the support of the baby's father.

The former honors student had to drop out of high school because of incessant morning sickness. Old friends distanced themselves from her when they learned she was pregnant. In time, she overcame depression and earned her G.E.D. with her mother's ongoing support and encouragement.

Morales also got help from Opportunities for a Better Tomorrow, a job placement center where she received job training and placement.

Though the road has been tough at times, Morales finds joy in her role as a mom. She works hard and continues to set goals for herself and her toddler.

Deal positively with the challenges and choices you face.

Inspired decisions are on the lips of a king; his mouth does not sin in judgment. (Proverbs 16:10)

Give us Your strength to do what is right, no matter the cost, Merciful Father, and to support all who are trying to do the same.

Making the Sick More Comfortable

A recent study sheds light on the effects of end-of-life care, indicating that palliative care can help make patients with terminal diseases more comfortable and perhaps lengthen their lives.

Palliative care, or any form of medical or alternative treatment that aims to reduce the severity of disease symptoms, has captured the attention of the medical community in recent years.

Conducted by the *New England Journal of Medicine,* the study shows that patients who receive palliative care early on—as soon as a diagnosis is made—typically live nearly three months longer than patients receiving only standard care, such as chemotherapy.

Although experts have not yet pinpointed why palliative care tends to extend life, some have a theory: patients whose pain is treated tend to sleep better, eat better and interact more with others. Severe pain, on the other hand, can contribute to depression and seclusion.

Every day of life is precious; treat it as such.

May the Lord of peace Himself give you peace. (2 Thessalonians 3:16)

Cloak the suffering with comfort, Holy Spirit.

Made In America

In today's suffering American economy, many manufacturers and businesses feel threatened by the amount of foreign imports. As a result, Elma, New York, welder Mark Andol created a store called Made in America which features an array of goods, every last part of which is fashioned in the United States.

Initially, Andol was doubtful as to how well his products would sell. Happily, his grand opening last year brought in 800 people.

"Everyone was shaking my hand and crying," Andol said in the *New York Post*. "Everyone lost trust in the system. This gave them hope."

Andol's business began with 50 products and has now expanded to 3,000. He has high hopes that his number of store products will continue to increase, and looks forward to opening up locations in Florida, Tennessee, Texas and New York City.

Do you have any creative ideas that could benefit your community or country?

Whatever your task, put yourselves into it, as done for the Lord. (Colossians 3:23)

Lord, may we remember every nation stands firm with You as its leader.

Health Report Cards

Knowledge is power and it can also be an important motivator for change.

The Robert Wood Johnson Foundation and the University of Wisconsin's Population Health Institute released "County Health Rankings: Mobilizing Action Toward Community Health," which includes data on almost all of the nation's more than 3,000 counties.

The report considers health outcomes (disease and death rates) and health factors. These include obesity rates, tobacco use, alcohol consumption, unemployment, income, community safety, access to health care and environmental factors.

You can go on the Web and see how different U.S. counties compare in terms of health scores. At least one county was shocked into action when residents learned they were rated very low. They've since made changes to improve things.

Fortified with knowledge, you can take on the challenge of making healthy lifestyle changes.

Do you not know that your bodies are members of Christ? (1 Corinthians 6:15)

Guide me in making healthy choices for my own welfare and that of my family, Eternal One.

A Valuable and Important Life

Best-selling author Dean Koontz has sold more than 400 million copies of his books worldwide. Even more admirably, he uses his work to be a champion for the disabled by creating characters—often children—who have special needs like autism or Down Syndrome.

Koontz and his wife, Gerda, have long worked with a charity called Canine Companions for Independence which trains service dogs for people with disabilities. As a result, they saw that disabled children are often shunned and looked on as if they have nothing to contribute to society. These experiences inspired the author to include characters with disabilities in his stories to highlight both their capabilities and their dignity.

In an interview on our *Christopher Closeup* radio show/podcast, Koontz explained, "I've never found [a disabled person]…who wasn't grateful for every good thing that comes their way. And I haven't found one that wasn't an inspiration to people. If you can inspire other people by your own courage, you've had a very valuable life."

Don't define people by their disabilities. Remember that each of us has a God-given purpose and is worthy of love.

Live in love, as Christ loved us. (Ephesians 5:2)

Lord, help me see Your presence in all people.

Talking to God

Archbishop Francois Fenelon was a great spiritual thinker in 17th-century France. He once wrote these words on the subject of prayer:

"Tell God all that is in your heart as one unloads one's heart to a dear friend.

"Tell Him your troubles that He may comfort you; tell Him your joys that He may sober them; tell Him your longings that He may purify them; tell Him your dislikes that He may help you conquer them.

"Talk to Him of your temptations that He may shield you from them. Show Him all the wounds of your heart that He may heal them.

"Blessed are they who attain such familiar, unreserved communion with God."

God is always available when His children need Him. Take advantage of His constant, loving presence.

Then the priests and the Levites stood up and blessed the people, and their voice was heard; their prayer came to His holy dwelling in heaven. (2 Chronicles 30:27)

Thank You for always being attentive to my prayers, Savior.

Going the Distance—In Good Health

A noted comic once quipped, "I don't want to grow old, but I sure don't like the alternative." Few of us relish the thought of growing older, but experts say our outlook can actually determine how well we age. Because the body's needs change with age, aging well requires an understanding of how to adjust our lives accordingly. Simple steps to aging well include:

- Fuel up wisely. Go for healthier food choices and focus on nutrition, variety and healthful alternatives.

- Stay fit. As we age, our heart, lungs and other internal organs change. This doesn't mean, however, that one should become sedentary. It means we need to exercise smarter, more prudently—but exercise, nonetheless.

- Reset your outlook. A positive attitude is necessary to successful aging, say experts. Evidence abounds supporting the link between a positive outlook and good health.

Staying positive helps us in many ways, so make an effort to stay upbeat.

Even to old age and gray hairs, O God, do not forsake me, until I proclaim Your might to all the generations to come. (Psalm 71:18)

Guide us through life's changes with Your grace, Lord.

Yes — Touch the Art!

The Vatican Museums now offer a hands-on approach to art for the blind and visually impaired—literally.

Special tours provide a multi-sensory experience of some of the Museums' most famous works. For example, to examine Michelangelo Merisi Caravaggio's "Deposition From the Cross," visitors first listen to a related biblical passage, to Gregorian chant with connected lyrics and to a brief account of the artist's life.

Then, each visitor's hands are placed on a resin bas relief of the scene. By guiding the person's hands across every detail, explains Isabella Salandri, who is in charge of such tours, they create a mental picture of how the many faces and limbs are arranged. "Like a puzzle," she says.

There are many ways to "see" what surrounds us. Always look at life with a full heart.

I will lead the blind by a road they do not know, by paths they have not known I will guide them. (Isaiah 42:16)

This day, Lord, help me to see—and serve— You in my neighbor.

Letting Go of Worries

In *The Little Book of Letting Go,* author Hugh Prather has the following to say about worrying:

"We think that those who worry are more empathetic and socially responsible. We believe that our angst demonstrates our concern that so many people in the world are suffering.

"But does worrying connect us to these people? Does it heal anyone? Worry is a fear state, and fear is tentative and uncommitted. It causes our mind to withdraw, turn in on itself, and shrink.

"As the Bible and other sacred Scriptures point out, the strong unifying force of Love has within it no aspect of fear."

Though it's normal to feel worried from time to time, some people have turned it into a habit that dominates their lives. As a result, it negatively affects their mental, emotional, and spiritual health—and possibly the health of the people around them as well.

Remember, we're all called to trust God. He will help us bear our burdens.

There is no fear in love, but perfect love casts out fear; for fear has to do with punishment, and whoever fears has not reached perfection in love. (1 John 4:18)

Help me grow in love, Divine Savior.

Voluntary Poverty

In her book *Mother Teresa and Me: Ten Years of Friendship,* author Donna-Marie Cooper O'Boyle recalls the first time she visited the Missionaries of Charity convent in Harlem, New York, for a retreat. She slept in their shelter for homeless women, and assisted with various tasks during her stay.

It was a poorer setting than O'Boyle was used to, and it left her feeling humble and appreciative of the blessings in her life. She also learned another valuable lesson from the experience.

O'Boyle writes, "Mother Teresa and the sisters believed that they could not serve the poor properly if they did not live exactly as the poor themselves. In her marvelous wisdom, she also knew that voluntary poverty does not constrain; on the contrary, it liberates. It frees a person of attachments to, and care for, material things. Because of this, he or she can focus on what is truly essential: God and neighbor."

Be attentive to God and your neighbors today.

Those who despise their neighbors are sinners, but happy are those who are kind to the poor. (Proverbs 14:21)

Help me see Your presence in my neighbor, Father.

Practicing Selfless Love

When we minister to someone who is suffering and dying, a part of us suffers and dies along with that person. But at the same time, another part of us grows.

We develop our capacity to practice love in its most selfless form—to put someone else's comfort and well-being ahead of our own.

So along with the pain, we experience the joy of selfless giving. And in so doing, we find a reflection of God's love for us.

The greatest riches of this life are found in our relationships with other people and with God. There will be both good times and bad. But together, they create something that is truly divine.

When Jesus arrived, He found that Lazarus had already been in the tomb four days...When Mary came where Jesus was and saw Him, she knelt at His feet and said to Him, "Lord, if you had been here, my brother would not have died." When Jesus saw her weeping...He was greatly disturbed in spirit and deeply moved. (John 11:17, 32-33)

Through the pain of grief and loss, help us feel Your comforting presence, Jesus, so that we can grow in love.

Failure Isn't Fatal

Bonnie Hunt has become a successful actress, writer, director, and talk-show host. But there was a time when she was unsure of what path to follow in life.

For several years, she worked as a nurse in the cancer ward of a Chicago hospital. She also harbored dreams of an acting career. When her patients found out, they encouraged her to shoot for the stars.

Hunt recalls, "I had all these patients—some of them my own age—with a limited amount of time to live. And they'd say to me, 'Whatever it is you want to do, just go do it. And don't be afraid of failure. That can't hurt anybody.'"

With the prodding of her first "real fans," Bonnie Hunt pursued and achieved her goal.

There may be some risk involved in following our dreams. But remember that failure isn't fatal. So give your goals the opportunity to flourish.

I press on toward the goal for the prize of the heavenly call of God in Christ Jesus. (Philippians 3:14)

Replace my fear with trust in You, Father.

These Are Not Disposable People

In his book *A Crime So Monstrous: Face-to-Face with Modern-Day Slavery,* author E. Benjamin Skinner shares the story of Bill, a boy in Haiti who was taken in as a domestic slave after his mother died. Bill was often beaten until strips of flesh came off his back.

A nun named Sister Caroline, who had been acquainted with Bill's mother, heard about his situation. She hired two men to rescue him, then placed him in St. Joseph's Home for Boys in Port-au-Prince which provided him with a loving home. Many years later, Bill became the manager of that home in order to help other boys in desperate situations.

On our *Christopher Closeup* radio show/podcast, Skinner said, "The degree to which individuals like Bill can take their lot in life...then go make the world a better place really underscores why it's worth fighting slavery. These aren't disposable people; these are people that can be survivors—and these survivors can be leaders and radically scale up the degree to which their communities understand liberty."

Pray for those dealing with persecution.

Hate evil and love good, and establish justice. (Amos 5:15)

Help me be a voice for liberty, Savior.

Blessed Brew

While the familiar coffee smell may permeate the air surrounding a monastery in Wyoming, even more powerful is the presence of the Carmelite Brothers who live and work there.

The monks have seen a growth in sales of the coffee they produce—Mystic Monk Coffee—with orders from as far away as New Zealand. The coffee beans are imported, then blended at the monastery.

According to one neighbor, the Carmelite coffee business has blessed the surrounding community, providing employment and offering a model for daily living. "The example of their lives dedicated to prayer and serving God cannot help but affect all who come into contact with them," the neighbor said.

No matter what our "day job" may be, it can always be done in a spirit of hope and love for others.

You will be enriched in every way for your great generosity, which will produce thanksgiving to God through us. (2 Corinthians 9:11)

May Your love, Eternal Father, fill our hearts and bring us peace.

A Saint's Example

Robert Bolt's play, *A Man For All Seasons*, tells the story of St. Thomas More, the Lord Chancellor of England who was executed by Henry VIII in 1535 for refusing to approve of the King's divorce and his decree that the country would no longer be connected to the Catholic Church.

While some believed that More should go against his faith and support Henry, the future saint held firm to his beliefs. In Bolt's story, he speaks the line, "When statesmen forsake their own private conscience for the sake of their public duties, they lead their country by a short route to chaos."

That's a noteworthy statement because it applies not only to statesmen, but to all human beings. Conscience is more than a personal matter; it's God's way of conforming us to His will.

Our words and actions affect others. If we choose popularity over principles, the people who look to us as an example will be led astray. But when we hold to our convictions, we strengthen our moral sense and become better human beings.

I hold fast my righteousness, and will not let it go; my heart does not reproach me for any of my days. (Job 27:6)

Strengthen my convictions, Jesus.

The Power of School Supplies

Academy Award-nominated actor and *CSI: NY* star Gary Sinise visited Iraq in 2003 to support the U.S. military. He saw that troops had been helping locals rebuild their schools.

When Sinise returned home, he started collecting school supplies at his children's school and sending them to Iraq to help out. After discovering that *Seabiscuit* author Laura Hillenbrand also had an interest in helping Iraqi kids, the two teamed up to create a charity called Operation Iraqi Children.

Since 2004, they've sent 300,000 school supply kits, soccer balls, shoes, blankets and other items over to the troops so that they could go into villages and hand them out.

On our *Christopher Closeup* radio show/podcast, Sinise said, "We've had kids run out and stop a convoy because a bomb had been placed on the road. This was a village that was previously hostile, but then these supplies were handed out and now it's a friendly village... And, of course, the supplies help the kids."

Even in times of war, simple acts of kindness can make a difference on the road toward peace.

Righteousness exalts a nation. (Proverbs 14:34)

May Your Holy Spirit bring us peace, Jesus.

Healing in Bloom

According to Susannah Felts in *Spry* magazine, garden therapy may be a relatively new method of medical healing, but it's an effective one used by hospitals around the country to improve mobility and ease depression.

One 2007 study indicates that gardening is especially beneficial for seniors and psychiatric patients. "There's a big emotional benefit to nurturing a living thing," claims horticultural therapist Teresia Hazen.

Every human being wants to feel needed and useful. Gardening can serve as a handy outlet in which one can create beauty and a comforting emotional space at the same time.

"Seeing flowers, touching plants...stimulates our brains in ways that make us feel better," observes landscape designer Naomi Sachs, founder of the Therapeutic Landscapes Network.

Take a minute from the stresses of everyday life to drink in the natural beauty that is God's creation. You may find yourself greatly rejuvenated in more ways than one.

Praise the Lord from the earth. (Psalm 148:7)

Jesus, in adding to the beauty of Your world, may we find ourselves both emotionally and spiritually strengthened.

Resting, But Not Idle

Call it what you will: daydreaming, letting your mind wander, or wasting time. Most of us would agree that letting our thoughts drift aimlessly is usually a less-than-productive use of our time.

Scientists, however, see such activity differently. In fact, daydreaming represents an important, purposeful activity for the brain's health and well-being and could even provide clues to common brain disorders and, subsequently, their cures.

Individually, the brain has "regions" that provide humans the ability to remember and daydream about the past, components that hold important roles. However, when these structures operate in unison, the brain seems to enter a "default" mode, a state that scientists are beginning to believe lends insight into diseases such as Alzheimer's, autism and depression—and ultimately, a cure.

What memories of the past do you hold dear? Share them so as to keep them alive.

I remember the days of old, I think about all Your deeds, I meditate on the works of Your hands. (Psalm 143:5)

Enable us to remember the past and learn from it, Father.

Holy Ground

In her Christopher Award-winning book entitled *Standing on Holy Ground,* author Sandra E. Johnson chronicles a modern day tale of racial hatred and harmony.

In 1985, St. John the Baptist church in Dixiana, South Carolina was vandalized by the KKK. That's when two friends—one white, one black—rallied volunteers to restore the church. Hundreds of people from diverse racial and cultural backgrounds responded to their call.

Despite repeated attempts on their lives, and even after the church was burned down in a hate-crime epidemic, these volunteers stayed committed to renovating and rebuilding God's house.

Remember that courageous hearts can turn hateful actions into moments of redemption and grace.

Whoever says, "I am in the light," while hating a brother or sister is still in the darkness. Whoever loves a brother or sister lives in the light. (1 John 2:9)

Help us see past superficial differences, Lord, and realize that we are all made in Your image and likeness.

A Prayer For Soldiers

Today we'd like to share with you part of a prayer for soldiers written by Rabbi Jerome Epstein.

"God of love, God of peace, I stand before You with respect and concern for those who have been summoned to protect and secure our nation, our world.

"Give them the courage to meet the chilling stare of death. Show compassion to them as they seek to make the world safer for me and for those I love.

"Ease the pain of their loneliness as they face the darkness of their daunting task.

"Let them feel Your presence as You warm the chill of their souls with the blanket of Your light.

"Let them sense the yearning of those who await their return and long for their presence—their loved ones, their parents, their children.

"Protect them when they find themselves in harm's way. Salve their wounds with Your healing balm. Amen."

You have given me the shield of Your salvation, and Your right hand has supported me; Your help has made me great. (Psalm 18:35)

Guide and protect all those serving in the armed forces, Merciful Savior.

Stand and Deliver

Feeling a bit out of shape plugging away at a desk job that has you sitting hour after hour behind a computer? You're not alone.

Studies at the Mayo Research Clinic show that a sedentary job can lead to alarming health problems such as high cholesterol, diabetes, lower back pain, and thrombosis. Sitting too long can also cause excessive snoring because the fluid that sits in your legs all day moves to your neck at night, causing a condition called sleep apnea.

The solution to this widespread sitting epidemic? Stand up! Walk about an hour a day. Even when you're seated at a desk, move your body once in a while. Get up every half-hour or so to stretch your muscles.

Our bodies were made to move. People who do so are said to live longer, happier, and healthier lives. So what are you waiting for? Get moving!

While physical training is of some value, godliness is valuable in every way, holding promise for both the present life and the life to come. (1 Timothy 4:8)

Lord, help us to move both our bodies and our spirits to do Your will.

Nothing But the Truth

When he was younger, Mark indulged in both alcohol and marijuana. But after being arrested, he straightened out his life.

Years later, Mark became a top student at the New York City Police Academy. When his instructors asked if he'd ever used illegal drugs, he answered "no," thinking the truth would jeopardize his career.

Mark's superiors eventually learned about his marijuana use, and told him he would not become a police officer. The reason wasn't that he had used drugs—they were willing to forgive that mistake—but rather, that he had *lied* about it. "If you'd lie to us about something that's relatively small," they wondered, "can you be trusted in the bigger things?"

Mark now has a new career, along with a wife and young children. He makes it a point to teach his kids about honesty and the importance of good choices. Feeling content with his life, he admitted the lesson he learned: namely, "The truth does set us free!"

Truthful lips endure forever, but a lying tongue lasts only a moment. (Proverbs 12:19)

Give me the courage to always speak truth, Jesus.

Prayers, Prayers and More Prayers

In December 2010, Kelly Podraza of Omaha, Nebraska, lost her daughters, Jordyn, 12, and Taylor, 10, in a car accident.

In honor of her daughters' memories, Kelly established a dress-down fundraiser at her children's school, St. Wenceslaus. All proceeds from this monthly event are distributed to different charities, including the Ted E. Bear Hollow, a center that helps young people cope with grieving.

Since both Jordyn and Taylor were volleyball players, over $1,300 was also raised and allotted for the Eastern Nebraska Wheelchair Athletic Association.

Kelly says that without her faith in God, she never would have survived. "Prayers, prayers, and more prayers seem to be what's helping," she told the *Catholic Voice,* newspaper of the Omaha Archdiocese. "The thousands of people that attended the girls' wake and funeral touched my heart so deeply...Thank you."

Even when the outlook seems bleak, God is there to help restore your suffering spirit.

Then the Lord said, "I have observed the misery of my people...I know their sufferings and I have come down to deliver them." (Exodus 3:7-8)

God, help us to trust in our faith during times of sorrow.

Facebook and Friendship

There are many benefits to having a Facebook account. For example, it's an excellent way to keep in touch with faraway family and friends. As varied a community as Facebook offers, however, remember to extend your faith and friendships beyond the online realm.

As reported in the *Orthodox Observer* newspaper, a study revealed that teens often face depression because "the pressures of popularity, attention, and self-esteem are extending to the digital realm."

Additionally, says the newspaper, teens should remember that Facebook, like any online means of communication, "is not a moral-free or consequence-free zone." Words spoken can never be taken back, so never post anything that you wouldn't say in person. And don't be afraid to "defriend" someone who is constantly posting negative remarks on your wall.

On Facebook—and in life—friends should be a positive source of comfort and influence. God understands that our friends are our second family and, therefore, asks that we choose them wisely.

A friend loves at all times. (Proverbs 17:17)

Jesus, help us to be discerning and faithful in our friendships.

Frontline Faith

It can be difficult to feel connected to God when you're fighting on the front lines of an overseas war.

As a result, the Frontline Faith Project was established by Cheri Lomonte in 2009 to recharge soldiers' spiritual batteries by providing them with MP3 players filled with religious messages. Since then, it has streamed these messages of hope to over 7,000 members of the military.

Many soldiers fighting in Afghanistan have acknowledged that they suffer from the absence of their faith communities. They're grateful to organizations like Frontline Faith which help rekindle the spark of belief within them.

"[It's like] somebody is by your side to remind you that there's a higher purpose…to make your hardships seem relatively small and to remind you of your core beliefs," explains Lt. Loris Lapri of the U.S. Army's 2nd Cavalry Division.

The Lord is our most powerful ally in times of war. Lean on His strength and you will find yourself physically, emotionally and spiritually revived.

The name of the Lord is a strong tower; the righteous run into it and are safe.
(Proverbs 18:10)

Divine Savior, guide us in all of our battles.

For the Glory of God Alone

The great composer Johann Sebastian Bach dedicated each of his works to "the glory of God alone."

That's because Bach's main ambition was to serve as an instrument that would reflect God's glory to the people around him.

Little did he dream that this inspiring objective would draw out of him the power of composing beautiful music. Bach not only reached the people he worked with as music director in a German church. He reached the world—including generations that he would never personally know.

Bach's purpose and motivation were to love God above all else, and to love his neighbor because he saw in him the image of the Almighty.

When you use your gifts to glorify God and to help other people, you too will be creating a legacy that lasts beyond your lifetime.

O magnify the Lord with me, and let us exalt His name together. (Psalm 34:3)

Praise and honor to You, Heavenly Father.

Blindsided by Hope

Sean and Leigh Anne Tuohy are the real-life couple who were portrayed by Tim McGraw and Sandra Bullock in the Christopher Award-winning movie *The Blind Side*.

The film tells the story of an African-American teen named Michael Oher who grew up surrounded by drugs, violence and a lack of stability. A meeting with the Tuohys—a well-to-do white couple whose son and daughter attended Briarcrest Christian School in Memphis, Tennessee—led Michael to become a part of their family. They championed his education, and nurtured his talent for football that led him to the NFL.

Though some people might see Michael's crossing paths with the couple as luck, Leigh Anne Tuohy attributes the whole situation to God. She said on *Christopher Closeup*, "We don't believe in coincidence...We believe it has been God-driven from the very beginning, and that the Lord had...a reason for this happening...There are kids that need help; our foster care system needs to be improved; there are kids that need adopting—and we are going to talk about it because we think it's that important."

I will not leave you orphaned; I am coming to you. (John 14:18)

Nurture our compassion, Lord.

The Cherokee Language

In the early 1800s, an illiterate man named Sequoyah watched in awe as white settlers made marks on paper, convinced that these "talking leaves" were the source of their power. This inspired the half-white, half-Cherokee whose English name was George Gist to create a written Cherokee language.

Sequoyah began devising a writing system for the spoken Cherokee language. Despite the ridicule of friends who thought he was crazed, within 10 years he had created 85 simple characters, each representing a distinct sound. Combinations of the symbols spelled words.

Within a few years, Cherokees had adopted this system, and Sequoyah became a folk hero as the inventor of the first Native American script in North America.

When the going gets tough, consider the obstacles other people have had to overcome throughout history. It just might put your struggles into perspective.

He has filled him with divine spirit, with skill, intelligence, and knowledge in every kind of craft. (Exodus 35:31)

Bless those who are native to our nation, Almighty God.

Thankful For Laughter

Thanksgiving is a time to appreciate the blessings of family and friends—and hopefully have a few laughs. Here's a poem that might give you a chuckle:

"May your stuffing be tasty, May your turkey be plump, May your potatoes and gravy have nary a lump.

"May your yams be delicious, And your pies take the prize, And may your Thanksgiving dinner stay off your thighs!"

There's also an amusing story about an eight-year-old girl named Jolene who was helping her Mom serve dessert after Thanksgiving dinner. She brought her father a piece of pumpkin pie to enjoy, but he gave it to one of their guests. Jolene got a second piece of pie, gave it to her father, then watched as he passed it to another guest. After bringing out the third piece of pie and watching her Dad give it away, Jolene finally exclaimed, "It's no use, Daddy. The pieces are all the same size!"

Be sure to share some funny stories of your own at the Thanksgiving table.

Worship the Lord with gladness; come into His presence with singing...Enter His gates with thanksgiving. (Psalm 100:2,4)

Teach me to appreciate the blessings of laughter, Lord.

In Humble Thanksgiving

Msgr. Raymond Balzer's faith, kindness and gratefulness of heart have shaped the lives of many throughout his priesthood.

Approaching his ministry in the Diocese of Fort Wayne-South Bend, Indiana, as a "pledge of service," he has always been willing to make sacrifices in order to embody God's love to others.

On the occasion of his 50th anniversary as a priest, Msgr. Balzer cited teaching schoolchildren, ministering to the sick and shut-ins, and celebrating Mass as the most satisfying parts of his job. He also enjoyed returning to his hometown of Beaver Falls, Pennsylvania, every Thanksgiving and taking his cousins, nieces, and nephews on a hike so the family members doing the cooking could finish their work in peace.

Reflecting on the past, Msgr. Balzer pondered the line from Psalms which asks, "How can I repay the Lord for all the good done for me?" His response: "Everyone knows we can't repay the Lord. All we can do is bow our head in humble thanksgiving."

I will raise the cup of salvation and call on the name of the Lord. (Psalms 116:13)

Help us live with gratitude, Lord.

A Prayer of Thanksgiving

Rev. Samuel F. Pugh once wrote a Thanksgiving prayer that can help us appreciate the blessings in our lives, and recognize the hardships experienced by many:

"O God, when I have food, help me to remember the hungry;

"When I have work, help me to remember the jobless;

"When I have a home, help me to remember those who have no home at all;

"When I am without pain, help me to remember those who suffer;

"And remembering, help me to destroy my complacency, bestir my compassion, and be concerned enough to help—by word and deed—those who cry out for what we take for granted.

"Amen."

As the holiday season begins, open your mind and heart to the challenges faced by the people in your family, church, or community—and do all that you can to help.

You will be enriched in every way for your great generosity, which will produce thanksgiving to God through us. (2 Corinthians 9:11)

Thank You, Lord, for all the blessings in my life.

A Winner On — and Off — the Football Field

Most people know Kurt Warner as the former NFL quarterback and Super Bowl champion who played for the St. Louis Rams and the Arizona Cardinals. Now Warner spends much of his time helping people in need.

Warner and his wife, Brenda, founded the First Things First foundation, a charitable organization that conducts broad outreach efforts to the needy.

The organization raised more than $675,000 for victims of the 2008 Midwest floods, has shipped hundreds of care packages to troops overseas, and sponsors Disney World trips for seriously ill children and their families.

The couple takes a personal interest in their charitable efforts. Each year, they and their children stuff Christmas stockings with gifts which they deliver to an agency that helps needy children.

Each of us can take some time to reach out to others who need our compassion.

Sing for joy, O heavens, and exult, O earth...For the Lord has comforted His people, and will have compassion on His suffering ones. (Isaiah 49:13)

Remind me that I am my brother's keeper, Jesus, my Savior.

Singing Shoppers

On one recent weekend in the holiday season, shoppers in a Pennsylvania department store paused for a moment to enjoy a song.

Some 650 singers from the Opera Company of Philadelphia who were scattered throughout the crowds suddenly burst into Handel's *Hallelujah Chorus,* surprising and delighting all.

The event was part of "Random Acts of Culture," a series that brings classical artists out of the performance halls and into the streets and everyday lives. The Knight Foundation plans to produce 1,000 such "random acts" over a three-year period in eight U.S. cities.

"Not everyone can make it to see an opera, or the ballet," says Dennis Scholl, Vice President of Arts at Knight Foundation. "But when you get a taste of it—even for just a few minutes—you feel the magic."

Every day is filled with moments that lighten our hearts, bringing joy to our lives. Enjoy them!

It was the duty of the trumpeters and singers to make themselves heard in unison in praise and thanksgiving to the Lord. (2 Chronicles 5:13)

When I am downcast, Father, send me Your joy.

Sign of Peace

A young man, age 19, had recently lost several people who were close to him, including his father and his best friend.

One day, when he was feeling despondent, he went to Mass, but sat off to the side and barely participated.

The young man recalls that at the sign of peace, when people traditionally acknowledge each other with a handshake, something special happened.

"Two elderly women," he said, "hobbled over to my solitary corner on fragile legs. Their journey seemed to take forever, and yet their greeting was warm and caring. In the time it took them to arrive, I made the decision to rejoin the living."

We take it for granted that if a word or gesture is small to us, then other people feel the same. But remember, sometimes it's the little acts of kindness that can have the biggest effect.

As God's chosen ones, holy and beloved, clothe yourselves with compassion, kindness, humility, meekness, and patience. (Colossians 3:12)

Open my eyes to see the people around me who are in need of loving acts of kindness, Lord.

Cultivating Hope

What is it about a 10-acre garden in England that brings visitors from far and wide each February? Perhaps it's the promise of new life.

During winter's dreariness, people are drawn to Colesbourne Park to enjoy the honey-scented fragrance of thousands of blooming snowdrops (from the genus *galanthus*) which are a harbinger of spring.

"We get an amazing mix of visitors, from titled people to plumbers, all sharing a common love of snowdrops," says nursery owner Joe Sharman, who runs annual Galanthus Galas around the country. "The galas get information out to a wider audience than traditional snowdrop parties and teas."

Sharman points out that the snowdrop is "the first flower of the year and no matter how miserable it is, spring is coming."

Hope is a vital emotion. Nurture it along with the flowers in your garden.

The flowers appear on the earth; the time of singing has come. (Song of Solomon 2:12)

Divine Lord, thank You for the beauty of nature and the reminder of hope that Your wonders offer us.

Learning About God—From Dogs

A recent statistic revealed that more than 74 million dogs are part of American households. As companions and helpers, they offer happiness and, some suggest, insight into how we relate to God.

- Staying close. Dogs want to be close to us; they'll even jump when they see us to get as near to us as they can. Do we pray often and deeply enough to draw closer to God?

- Getting the message. Watch a dog—head-twisting, ear-twitching—trying to understand us. Do we try to discern what God is telling us to do?

- Taking comfort. Dogs may cry in the face of a storm, forcing their way into our laps to feel safe. Do we trust in God's promise that He is with us always, and so we should never fear?

The knowledge of God's boundless love should fill our every day with joy.

Trust in the Lord with all your heart, and do not rely on your own insight. In all your ways acknowledge Him, and He will make straight your paths. (Proverbs 3:5-6)

Spirit of Love, You give me all good things, and I offer You my thanks and praise.

Nod Off, Power On

An afternoon nap could make you more productive.

At least that's what psychologists at the University of California, Berkeley, have concluded. They gave two groups of adults a learning test designed to stimulate a part of the brain critical to short-term memory.

Two hours after taking the test, one group was allowed a nap for 90 minutes; the other continued to work. At day's end, the test was administered again, with the group that had napped scoring markedly better than the one denied rest.

Just as sleeping seems to "reboot" the brain, taking a break from the day's activities to focus on the stillness of God's presence around us and within us can refresh the soul. Chances are that all our souls could use some refreshing, so put aside some quiet time to spend with God.

Be still and know that I am God! I am exalted among the nations, I am exalted in the earth. (Psalm 46:10)

In the silence, I listen for Your call, ready to do Your will, Father of all.

The Life Behind the Story

Few of us can say that one single story "defines" us. Yet, Art Huser of Indianapolis may well be entitled to that claim.

Years ago, a major storm hit Indiana, dumping several feet of snow on Huser's area. Relatives tried to reach the then 80-something Huser, who didn't answer his phone. As the wind howled and blizzard conditions worsened, concerned family members went to Huser's house, only to find him in his barn, at 10 pm, feeding his lambs.

Neighbors and family enjoy this story, which came to sum up Huser's hospitality, love of animals and joy of caring for the vulnerable and helpless.

In fact, Huser maintains that caring for his sheep is part of what's kept him living well into his 90s. "I tell you, those sheep have kept me healthy," he says. "I feel good after I take care of my sheep."

We build up God's kingdom and our own sense of purpose when we care for others. Be a good shepherd to someone today.

I am the good shepherd. The good shepherd lays down his life for the sheep. (John 10:11)

Day by day, You are my Shepherd, Lord Christ.

Moment to Shine

Frances McGee-Cromartie felt worried about her daughter Elizabeth, believing the eighth-grader had great potential, but wasn't assertive enough to display her many talents to the world. That worry peaked the night of her school's Christmas concert.

"The more I coaxed [Elizabeth] to take a step into the spotlight, the more she insisted on fading in the background," Cromartie recalled in *Guideposts* magazine. "Just once, I wanted her to have a moment to shine."

Another mother introduced herself to Cromartie and thanked her for Elizabeth's kindness to her son, an autistic eighth-grader. That kindness, she explained, made a tremendous difference in helping him feel better about himself and fitting in with the other kids.

A proud Cromartie then bore witness to the emergence of her own "shining star" as she introduced a smiling Elizabeth to the mother of the boy whose life she had so deeply influenced.

The Lord has graced us all with shining talents. Remember, you don't have to be in the spotlight to have your "moment to shine."

**Let your light shine before others.
(Matthew 5:16)**

May we use our God-given talents, Messiah.

The Value of Integrity

Many years ago, advertising executive Charles Brower made a number of pointed observations on the occasion of his retirement. A number of them had to do with "integrity."

First: Honesty is not only the best policy; it is rare enough today to make you pleasantly conspicuous.

Second: The expedient thing and the right thing are seldom the same thing.

Third: You cannot sink someone else's end of the boat and still keep your own afloat.

Fourth: A man of stature has no need of status.

Finally: Never trust a man who is Dr. Jekyll to those above him and Mr. Hyde to those under him.

A life of integrity requires courage, confidence and strength. Nourish these qualities in your daily life.

If you will walk before Me, as David your father walked, with integrity of heart and uprightness, doing according to all that I have commanded you...then I will establish your royal throne over Israel forever. (1 Kings 9:4-5)

Help me live according to Your principles, Lord.

A Generous Spirit

"Kristin loved children. She felt bad for kids who had nothing," said her grieving mother, Janet Zuerblis, who lost her young daughter to an aggressive form of liver cancer.

But Kristin's generous spirit lives on at St. Mark's church in Long Valley, New Jersey. As a 15-year-old, she created a project decorating her parish Christmas tree with handmade angel ornaments with the name of a disadvantaged child. Parishioners take ornaments off the tree and fulfill holiday gift wishes for each youngster.

Today, the project continues. At the top of the tree is an ornament with the picture of Kristin.

"We tell new Senior Youth Ministry members about Kristin," says the religious education director. "She loved the tradition and worked hard to make the tree beautiful."

A beautiful spirit lives on. Honor your deceased loved ones by helping other people in some appropriate way.

Jesus said, "Let the little children come to Me, and do not stop them." (Matthew 19:14)

Child of Bethlehem, may I see Your beautiful face in the face of each person I meet today.

An Accidental Journey

St. Francis Xavier, a famous 16th-century missionary to Asia, probably never dreamed of leaving his native Spain to preach the Gospel. He was content with scholarly pursuits at home.

In fact, he only went to India because another priest who had been selected for the journey became ill. At the last minute, St. Ignatius Loyola, who was heading up a newly formed order of priests to which Xavier belonged—the Society of Jesus, better known as the Jesuits—asked him to take the place of the ailing priest. On that day in 1541, Xavier unintentionally began his missionary service, work he continued until his death in 1552.

In our own lives, people may present opportunities we might not normally consider. We need to remain openly courageous to the good these experiences may bring into our lives—and the lives of those around us.

Those who know Your name put their trust in You, for You, O Lord, have not forsaken those who seek You. (Psalm 9:10)

Guide my steps, and give me direction, Holy Mighty One.

We Interrupt These Studies — For Prayer

What do students at the College of Wooster do after a day of taking final exams? Study more? Sleep? Well, both eventually, but first they pray.

The Catholic Student Association has provided a place where students of all religions can gather, relax and pray in a private room on campus.

"Exams have been rough," says Ana Capellin. "This helps reduce some of the stress."

Campus minister Karen Hahn credits students for the idea. "Our hope is to give students a break in the context of prayer," she explains, "a chance to reconnect with God and to savor a moment of peace in all the craziness."

It's always a good time for a prayer break—seeking help and hope from the Source of all wisdom, love and joy.

If any of you is lacking in wisdom, ask God, who gives to all generously and ungrudgingly, and it will be given you. But ask in faith, never doubting. (James 1:5-6)

Send me Your Spirit, Lord, that I may know Your will.

Small Wounds Hurt the Most

Have you ever wondered why superficial paper cuts often hurt worse than more serious wounds?

The reason, doctors tell us, is that sensory nerve endings are close to the skin and are especially numerous on the hands. So even though a paper cut doesn't do much damage, it irritates these sensitive nerve endings. As a result, we feel pain out of proportion to the injury.

Small cutting remarks from people close to us can also cause a disproportionate amount of pain. We are unusually sensitive to injury from those we love and respect. A small slight from them can be extremely painful.

Harsh words can cause damage that's more than skin deep. Let your voice be known for spreading kindness and praise.

Show yourself in all respects a model of good works, and in your teaching show integrity, gravity and sound speech that cannot be censured. (Titus 2:7-8)

Teach me to use my words to build others up, not tear them down, Holy Spirit.

The Kindness of Strangers

When Jim and Dylan began getting letters addressed to Santa Claus at their New York City apartment, they were confused as to why it was happening. After unsuccessful attempts at uncovering the source of the letters, they decided to focus on the hundreds of requests they were getting from children—things like Dora the Explorer cups for one girl's baby sister, and clothes with the exact size for another girl.

At first, Jim and Dylan felt it would be wrong to give presents to some kids, but not all of them. They began asking friends and strangers for help—taking the letters all over New York City, trusting people to keep their word and send a gift.

In the end, they got half the letters fulfilled, and a change of heart. Instead of worrying about not fulfilling all of the letters, Jim told the *New York Times,* "That is like saying, I can't fix all the world's problems, so I am not going to fix any of them." Dylan added, "Jim and I are only two elves, but we made a little dent."

How can you make a "little dent" and spread Christmas joy?

Ask and it will be given to you; seek and you will find; knock and the door will be opened to you. (Matthew 7:7)

Jesus, help us love children as You love them!

In the Eye of the Storm

When a powerful tornado hit the town of Sanford, North Carolina, the employees of a Lowe's Home Improvement Store remained surprisingly calm and focused on moving their 100 customers to the most secure corner of the store in the back of the building.

Gary Hendricks, one of the customers that day, told the *Today Show*, "One customer urged the others not to follow the employees to safety saying, 'That's not a tornado; you don't know what you're talking about.' When that man said that, it could have been a disaster…[Thankfully] one of the employee's said, 'Listen folks, let's not be stupid. Everyone head to the back of the store.'"

The Lowe's employees' persistence paid off. The corner of the store to which they had shepherded everybody was the only part of the building that wasn't destroyed. Everyone survived.

Life is full of storms that come from the outside and from within ourselves. How we react to them is what truly matters.

I would hurry to find a shelter for myself from the raging wind and tempest. (Psalm 55:8)

Steer me from stereotypes and snap judgments, Lord Jesus.

The Revelation of Christmas

In Greenville, Rhode Island, a small college celebrates the mystery of Christmas in a very personal way.

Each year, a group of students at Mater Ecclesiae College devotes several months to privately preparing the school's illuminated Christmas Room, an inspired work of art that includes a life-size nativity scene.

Typically, about 20 young women put their hearts and souls into the design, construction and decoration of the Christmas Room, which is closed off until Christmas Eve, when the display is revealed to the public.

Says one volunteer, "When working on this, I usually work in silence, and think about what it would have been like for the Blessed Mother to wait in silence for the birth of her son. It's working in prayer."

Take time for silent reflection each and every day. Insights and revelation come more easily when the soul is at rest.

Then Mary said, "Here am I, the servant of the Lord; let it be with me according to your word." (Luke 1:38)

Help still my soul, Prince of Peace.

The Lights of Hanukkah

One year during Hanukkah in Billings, Montana, a cinder block shattered the bedroom window of five-year-old Isaac Schnitzer. Its target: a menorah.

After discovering that a neo-Nazi group was responsible for the incident, the people of Billings displayed pictures of menorahs throughout the city.

When the Schnitzer family drove around their town, they saw menorahs on houses, storefronts and billboards.

Little Isaac said he didn't know so many people were Jewish. His mother responded, "They're not all Jewish, but they're all our friends."

The message of that Hanukkah was symbolized with light from candles—and celebrated with light from human beings. It just goes to show that the Christopher motto is true: "It's better to light one candle than to curse the darkness."

> **Then Judas and his brothers and all the assembly of Israel determined that every year at that season the days of dedication of the altar should be observed with joy and gladness for eight days. (1 Maccabees 4:59)**

Yahweh, remind us that we are all Your children.

Santa: The Next Generation

Tom Valent was already 25 years old when he decided he wanted to be none other than the jolly, generous Santa Claus.

For 10 years, Valent attended a Santa school in Midland, Michigan, not because he didn't get the hang of the work, but because it had a warm, friendly atmosphere. Today he runs the school, which draws 100 students a year from across the country. Classes touch on everything from Santa's history, to saying "Merry Christmas" in sign language, to diet suggestions.

Valent told *ABC News,* "We do try to teach the Santas that eating healthy is important. If you stay healthy, you're more alert, you're more up, and you can have a conversation…Children remember the conversation and the visit for a long time."

The most important Santa lesson of all, says Valent, is, "Never think you are the real Santa. It's a privilege, not a job."

The spirit of Santa Claus should live in all of us year-round. This Christmas season, be a Santa to everyone—and remember to take more pleasure in giving than receiving.

Receive the kingdom of God as a little child. (Luke 18:17)

Help us be models of generosity, Jesus.

Feeding the Human Spirit

Every weekday morning, volunteers from Holy Family Church in Omaha, Nebraska, make approximately 900 sack lunches to distribute to the homeless.

According to journalist Lisa Maxson, the lunch program has been running for four years—and the number of lunches required to feed the hungry has continued to increase. For the program's participants, the lunches do more than feed the body; they sustain the soul.

Jeremiah Young, who gets free lunches a few times a week, says, "It's so inspiring to come here each day. It's nice to see so many smiling faces...It just shows that good things can come even though you're at the bottom."

The volunteers also derive great benefits from their service. Fran Berg explains, "In Jesus' name, that's what we're supposed to be doing. We are to take care of the poor and the homeless...Once you do it, you'll find out it makes you feel as good as it does them."

Jesus taught that we should always give cheerfully to those in greater need. Even the smallest gift or effort can work wonders.

Help the weak. (1 Thessalonians 5:14)

Inspire me to give of myself, Lord.

Smoke Signals

A shipwreck survivor washed up on a small, deserted island. The man prayed to God for help, but no rescuers appeared.

Eventually he built a driftwood hut that protected him and kept him dry. But one day after scavenging for food, he returned to find his hut on fire.

He called out in despair, "God, how could you do this to me?"

The next day the man was stunned to see a ship coming to rescue him. "How did you know I was here?" he asked.

"We saw your smoke signal," they answered.

God is always at work in our lives, even in the midst of suffering. The next time your own hut seems to be burning to the ground, it just may be a smoke signal—one that summons the grace of God.

The Lord is near to all who call on Him, to all who call on Him in truth. He fulfills the desire of all who fear Him; He also hears their cry, and saves them. (Psalm 145:18-19)

Give me the vision to see Your will working in my life, Lord.

Giving Sight to the Blind

Twenty-nine-year-old tree trimmer John Wilkinson only had vision in one eye due to a sports injury he suffered as a teen. Though he had adjusted to that condition, his life took a downward turn when he suddenly lost vision in his good eye.

The Casselberry, Florida resident was diagnosed with a cataract, but didn't have health insurance. As reported in the *Orlando Sentinel,* Wilkinson became dependent on friends for everything.

One day, his seven-year-old niece told her Girl Scout leader, Jennifer Hicks, that her uncle's "eye was broken." Hicks took Wilkinson in to care for him, then contacted the Lions Club because they help people at risk of losing their eyesight. The Lions Club contacted Dr. David Auerbach who provided free cataract surgery to Wilkinson as a gesture of good will during the Christmas season.

Dr. Auerbach said, "There are so many mission trips, but we can stay and help in our own backyard."

Look around your "backyard" to see if you can share God's love with someone nearby.

He has sent Me to proclaim...recovery of sight to the blind. (Luke 4:18)

Enable me to help others see You more clearly, Lord.

Take a Chance on Faith

Actor Jim Caviezel (*The Passion of the Christ*) was always outspoken about his Christian beliefs. A friend challenged him to put his faith into action by adopting a disabled child.

That conversation led Caviezel and his wife, Kerri, to China where they adopted a five-year-old boy named Bo who suffered with a brain tumor. They supported Bo through dangerous brain surgery, and he is a valued member of their family today.

Caviezel and his wife then adopted another child—a five-year-old girl with a brain tumor. The couple had planned to adopt a healthy girl, but when they met the sick child, they realized that the healthy baby would find a good home; the sick one wouldn't.

When he was a guest on our *Christopher Closeup* radio show/podcast, Caviezel explained, "We took the harder road...That is what faith is to me; it's action. It's not the one who says he is; it's the one who does—and does without bringing attention to himself. I'm saying this because I want to encourage other people. Yes, you do feel scared, but you have no idea the blessings that you have coming to you if you just take a chance on faith."

Do not fear, I will help you. (Isaiah 41:13)

Help me to trust in You, Father.

A Prayer for Parents

Today we'd like to share with you a Christopher prayer for parents:

"Heavenly Father, You have given to men and women the awesome opportunity to participate in the creation of life. You've given them the opportunity to nurture their children, and to teach them the values and skills they will need as responsible creative adults.

"Bless fathers and mothers as they take on the joys and sorrows of parenthood. Enlighten them to communicate an awareness of those things that truly count.

"Strengthen them when they falter. Deepen their love for one another no less than for their children. Their love must know how to sacrifice—how to absorb friction and conflict. Their love is something special because it speaks of Yours. Amen."

He will turn the hearts of parents to their children, and the hearts of children to their parents. (Malachi 4:6)

Teach us to embody Your love for us, Heavenly Father, and direct it toward our children.

Angel for an Evening

Philip Stover and Father Charles Ehrenbach were strangers stranded at the Philadelphia Airport because of a blizzard-related delay in their flight to Albany, New York.

Stover noticed that the elderly priest looked confused. He asked if he needed help, discovered they were on the same flight, and the two men began a friendly conversation.

Once the plane took off and they arrived in Albany, Father Fehrenbach was stranded because his ride never showed up. Stover drove him to the hotel where the priest was scheduled to lead a retreat. After dropping him off, the shy Stover departed without saying good-bye.

A year later, Stover received a letter from Father Ehrenbach who said he believed his helper was an actual angel until he found his business card. Writing in *Catholic Digest*, Stover says the experience taught him that "we each have all it takes within us to become [God's] angel for an evening."

Reach out to someone in fellowship and you might find that you too can be "an angel for an evening."

Show hospitality. (Hebrews 13:2)

Lord, may we always give thanks for earthly angels.

An Interfaith Gesture at Christmas

Many years ago, Albert Rosen, a Jewish salesman in Milwaukee, decided to help a Christian better enjoy Christmas.

Rosen called the local newspapers and offered to fill in, without pay, for any Christian who was scheduled to work on Christmas Eve. He explained, "I see so many unfortunate people who aren't able to be with their families on Christmas Eve."

After receiving about a dozen calls, Albert decided to relieve a bartender who hadn't been home on Christmas Eve in nine years. Everyone experienced a happier holiday than expected.

The holiday season should be a time when faith and generosity abound. But we shouldn't just give material gifts; we should give of ourselves. Let's express our religious beliefs and concern for others through concrete, constructive action.

Do not store up for yourselves treasures on earth, where moth and rust consume and where thieves break in and steal; but store up for yourselves treasures in heaven...For where your treasure is, there will your heart be also. (Matthew 6:19-21)

Nurture in me a spirit of selfless giving, Yahweh.

The 12 Days of Christmas

With so much focus on December 25, we sometimes forget that the Christmas season doesn't end on Christmas Day, it begins then. Nick Wagner, writing in *U.S. Catholic*, makes some suggestions for a modern celebration of the 12 days of Christmas:

Wait until Christmas Eve to add the star to your tree. Mark St. Stephen's feast on December 26 by helping the poor, and St. John's feast the next day by reconciling with others. Make time for loved ones on the feast of the Holy Family—and revive a custom by praying the rosary on January 1.

Re-read the Christmas cards you received. Examine your conscience, confront injustice, and count your blessings. Share time with friends. Honor the Holy Name of Jesus on this feast. Observe the Epiphany by remembering the gifts of the Magi as well as the great gift of baptism.

Celebrate the entire Christmas season.

Where is the Child who has been born king of the Jews? For we observed His star at its rising, and have come to pay Him homage. (Matthew 2:2)

Child of Bethlehem, may I imitate the Wise Men and seek You with all my heart.

The Blessing of a New Family

Twenty-one-year-old Haylee Cain felt alone and hopeless. Afflicted with cerebral palsy which affects her arms and legs, her grandfather could no longer take care of her. She was placed in an Alabama nursing home for senior citizens.

Then, Michelle Eubanks of the Florence, Alabama, newspaper *The Times Daily,* wrote a story about Haylee's situation. Donna and Judson Emens, who had befriended Haylee when she was a young girl, saw the article and went to visit her. After seeing how sad Haylee appeared, the Emens decided to welcome her into their home. Their lives have been full of joy ever since.

During an interview on our *Christopher Closeup* radio show/podcast, program host Tony Rossi asked Donna where she got the courage to adopt someone with physical challenges.

She responded, "God inspired my life with my brother who had Down Syndrome. He died five years ago. I think God putting him in our lives helped us to realize that it's good to help other people with needs."

Ask what you can do to help others with special needs.

Whoever receives one such child in My name welcomes Me. (Mark 9:37)

Heal our loneliness with love, Divine Healer.

Children Should be Seen and Heard

According to *Catholic News Service's* David Gibson, children today need to be less ignored and better understood.

To this end, Gibson offers five brief but powerful truths regarding the importance of children:

1. Children possess great dignity; they are signs of God. Children embody Christ's image inside and outside of the Church.

2. Children frequently test their parents' patience. "Willfulness" is normal amongst young people and can be corrected.

3. Children suffer. A child can endure just as much pain as adults from difficulties such as disease, abuse, etc.

4. Children are growing. Children are in need of supportive environments in which to develop.

5. Each child is uniquely gifted. Help them discover their God-given talents.

The Lord exalts in the unique wonder of His children. As earthly parents and guardians, let us strive to better appreciate and enhance the glory and uniqueness of young people.

Do not neglect the gift that is in you.
(1 Timothy 4:14)

Messiah, may we strive to be more loving and understanding of our children.

Christmas for Forgotten Angels

Though Clarence Adams didn't know much about homelessness when he got a job as a counselor at a New Orleans, Louisiana, homeless shelter 17 years ago, he was especially moved by the plight of the children he saw there.

As Christmas drew near, he felt even more sorry for them because all they would have to look forward to is Christmas dinner in the shelter with hundreds of strangers. As reported by *Voice of America* news, Adams commented to a friend that if he ever got rich, he would have a big party for homeless children. His friend told him he didn't have to be rich; he could do something right away.

Though it involved a lot of work, Adams created the shelter's first Christmas for Forgotten Angels party. There was fried chicken, macaroni and cheese, dessert, and toys from Santa.

Adams recalls, "To see how much joy this brought to these children who would otherwise have nothing—I determined I had to do this every year."

You don't have to be rich to bring joy to someone in need.

Make [these] days of feasting and gladness. (Esther 9:22)

Inspire us to bring Your joy to others, Divine Messiah.

Divine Inspiration

George Frederick Handel lived to see his oratorio, *The Messiah,* become a cherished tradition. First performed in Ireland in 1742, the work achieved fame eight years later in London.

Few people realize, though, that this masterpiece was composed by Handel in 21 days during a desperate frenzy of inspiration. Hounded by creditors, he struggled against failing eyesight to finish what he felt would be his greatest work.

The composer's own suffering gave vibrancy and depth to the Messiah's theme: "Come unto me all ye that labor, and I will give you rest."

We admire artists and perhaps stand in awe of them because their efforts achieve a kind of immortality. But our deeds too can vibrate into eternity if they are motivated by love for God and people.

The kingdom of the world has become the kingdom of our Lord and of His Messiah, and He will reign forever and ever. (Revelation 11:15)

Turn my challenges and hardships into a means of praising You, Lord Jesus.

Christmas Keeps People Alive

When Elizabeth Scalia's brother was dying in a hospice in December, 2004, he read an article by a columnist denouncing Christmas. Despite his suffering, he responded to that article with a letter of his own that Scalia posted on her blog.

Her brother praised the doctors and nurses who took care of dying patients like himself, noting that none of them were as sour as this particular columnist.

He said, "Christmas, they will tell you, keeps people alive—even terribly, horrifically ill people alive—because it brings wonder, and it brings love, and love always brings hope. They will remind you that beyond Santa Claus and Frosty and going to the right parties, Christmas is a gathering of angels on a clear starry night...God condescends to join flawed, terrified, confused, sickened humanity—to confirm that life is worth living...He comes to say [that] love is worth dying for. It is worth living for, too, because the more you give away, the more you seem to get to keep."

The sights and sounds of Christmas should always remind us of the divine life that came into our world more than 2,000 years ago.

He is the image of the invisible God. (Colossians 1:15)

Lift our hearts so we can see Your presence, Jesus.

A Life Lesson for Christmas

Former *American Idol* contestant and Grammy-nominated gospel singer Mandisa remembers one Christmas when loneliness threatened to overcome her.

She was attending Fisk University in Nashville, Tennessee, and didn't have enough money to fly home for the holiday.

Instead of feeling depressed, the singer decided to spend Christmas day reading all the gospels so she could feel closer to Jesus. Ever since then, she's been able to focus on the religious significance of the holiday without getting too distracted by shopping, parties, and other activities. It also gave her a new perspective on the sadness some people feel during Christmas-time.

On *Christopher Closeup*, Mandisa told program host Tony Rossi, "When we think about why we celebrate Christmas and what Jesus came for, tears [of sadness] can be turned into tears of joy...God wipes away every tear from our eyes, so that gives me hope and encouragement."

May Christ's light illuminate your life this Christmas.

A Child has been born for us...and He is named Wonderful Counselor, Mighty God, Everlasting Father, Prince of Peace. (Isaiah 9:6)

Thank You, Jesus, for the precious gift of Yourself.

Finding God in Unexpected Places

Archbishop Fulton J. Sheen once shared these thoughts about Jesus' birth:

"[Joseph] searched for a place for the birth of Him to whom heaven and earth belonged... Certainly, thought Joseph, there would be room in the village inn. There was room for the rich; there was room for everyone who had a tip to give to the innkeeper. But when finally the scrolls of history are completed...the saddest line of all will be: *There was no room in the inn*.

"But there was room in the stable. The inn was the gathering place of public opinion...the rendezvous of the worldly, the rallying place of the popular and the successful. But there's no room in the place where the world gathers. The stable is a place for outcasts, the ignored and the forgotten. The world might have expected the Son of God to be born in an inn; a stable would certainly be the last place in the world where one would look for Him. The lesson is: divinity is always where you least expect to find it."

God is everywhere, so keep your eyes—and heart—open.

The Word became flesh. (John 1:14)

Thank You for sharing in our humanity, Divine Messiah.

A Little Thank You

In today's paper-less society, it's no small wonder that the art of writing thank-you notes has fallen to the wayside. Yet according to *CBS News* correspondent Steve Hartman, those who do take the time to write notes of gratitude consequently wind up feeling more grateful themselves.

It was ultimately *60 Minutes* correspondent Byron Pitts who convinced Hartman to try his hand at writing the forgotten "thank you." Pitts constantly pens thank-you letters to this day and continues to believe in the power of the printed note.

"There's something nice about the handwritten word, that people can feel it, touch it, you know?" Pitts told the doubtful Hartman.

When Hartman wrote his first thank-you note to his father-in-law, it was greatly appreciated.

A little thank-you note can go a long way in today's fast-paced world. Remember, the Lord rejoices in the gratitude of all His earthly children.

Give thanks to the Lord for His steadfast love endures forever. (2 Chronicles 20:21)

Lord, may we remember to thank those who fill our lives with joy and, above all, continually praise Your holy name.

Germs Like Worriers

"Worry is the interest we pay on trouble before it is due."

This is an old and true saying. If all the time and energy spent on fruitless worry could be channeled into positive and productive work, the world would be far better off than it is today.

People who are over-fearful, troubled or apprehensive bring much unnecessary misery into their own lives and the lives of those around them.

Worry not only takes away peace of mind, heart and soul, it harms the body as well. One doctor claimed that "germs like worriers." In other words, bacteria are more likely to infect people who tend to worry and fret.

Show a Christlike interest in those who brood and worry. Encourage them to shift from self-centered pursuits to the giving of themselves for others. Once they begin to experience the joy of helping others, their own problems will seem less important and may even disappear. Thus, gradually they will regain that sense of balance that Christ wishes all of us to possess.

Do not let your hearts be troubled, and do not let them be afraid. (John 14:27)

Let me be so concerned about the common good, O Lord, that I will not over-emphasize my own needs.

The Right to Believe

During the mid-1950's, a group of atheists demanded that the words "under God" be removed from the Pledge of Allegiance. New York State Supreme Court Judge Isadore Bookstein ruled against the atheists.

He stated that while the First Amendment guaranteed a citizen's "right to disbelieve," it gave the disbeliever "no preference over those who do believe in God."

Judge Bookstein wrote, "[The First Amendment] was conceived to prevent and prohibit the establishment of a state religion; it was not intended to prevent or prohibit the growth and development of a religious state."

To grant the request of the atheists, the Supreme Court Justice pointed out, "would be preferring those who believe in no religion over those who believe," and would invalidate the President's oath of office, the Declaration of Independence, and the oath of the court, all of which invoke God.

The battle to acknowledge God in the public square continues today. Exercise your right to believe.

Trust in the Lord with all your heart...In all your ways acknowledge Him. (Proverbs 3:5,6)

Let me show enthusiasm in honoring You, Lord.

Dreams Fulfilled

Vonetta Flowers competed for a spot in the 2000 Summer Olympics. Plagued with knee and ankle injuries, Flowers didn't make the finals in the track division. Then her husband heard about bobsledders looking for sprinters to train for the Winter Games because they needed people with certain athletic skills who could give a running push to the bobsled to start the race.

Though she tried out only half-seriously, Flowers showed potential, and was invited to train with the team. Being both fast and strong, she proved to be a valuable asset.

In the first-ever women's bobsled competition in the Olympics, Vonetta Flowers became the first African-American to win a gold medal at a Winter Games.

Adaptation and change can be both scary and painful. But they can also lead to the fulfillment of dreams. Pray for the wisdom to see where God is leading you.

[Make] your ear attentive to wisdom and [incline] your heart to understanding...cry out for insight, and raise your voice for understanding...then you will...find the knowledge of God.
(Proverbs 2:1-5)

Enable me, Spirit of Wisdom, to find You.

The Power to Give

It's said that it's better to give than to receive. But what happens when you feel even what you *do* give isn't enough?

The Salwen family had always been considered a generous clan. Parents Joan and Kevin volunteered for charities like Habitat for Humanity—and they joined their two children, Hannah and Joe, in working at a food shelter near their home in Atlanta, Georgia.

In spite of her family's contributions, 14-year-old Hannah still felt more could be done. Seeing a beggar on the street prompted Hannah to voice these concerns to her parents. Joan, her mother, eventually suggested selling their $2 million house and donating half of its worth to charity. The family actually agreed to do it.

As a result, the Salwens were ultimately able to give $800,000 to various charitable organizations. Not everyone is in the position to sell and donate half the profits of their homes. But it is Hannah Salwen's belief that "all Americans have the power to give something."

God instructs us to give freely and cheerfully, with no thought of compensation. Remember, gifts given in love are always appreciated.

Stretch out your hand to the poor. (Sirach 7:32)

Christ, may we never tire of selfless giving.

Going to Everyone with Love

Father James Keller, the founder of The Christophers, had this to say about the guiding principle behind the organization:

"The essence of being a Christopher—being a Christ bearer—is to do just what the Lord Himself did. He loved everybody. He loved even those who were against Him.

"The only people, as I see it, who show great daring today are people who love in a big way or hate in a big way. They want to reach the world.

"The Lord Himself said to go to everybody with His love. It's remained for our day that others have tried to go to everybody with hatred or destruction. But if you get another handful to be as daring—to go to all men with love—we can have a change in history."

Each of us has the power and responsibility to be a Christopher—to let our faith shine through our words and actions. Be that light in the darkness today and everyday.

Love one another with mutual affection; outdo one another in showing honor. (Romans 12:10)

Give me the wisdom, courage, strength, and patience to share Your love with everyone, Divine Savior.

Also Available

We hope that you have enjoyed *Three Minutes a Day, Volume 46*. These other Christopher offerings may interest you:

- **News Notes** are published 10 times a year on a variety of topics of current interest. Single copies are free; quantity orders available.

- **Appointment Calendars** are suitable for wall or desk and provide an inspirational message for each day of the year.

- **DVDs** range from wholesome entertainment to serious discussions of family life and current social and spiritual issues.

- **Website—www.christophers.org—**has *Christopher Closeup* radio programs, podcasts of *Christopher Minutes,* as well as uplifting stories, columns and other motivational material

For more information on The Christophers or to receive News Notes or a catalogue of additional material, please contact us:

The Christophers
5 Hanover Square
11th Floor
New York, NY 10004

Phone: 212-759-4050 / 888-298-4050
E-mail: mail@christophers.org
Website: www.christophers.org

The Christophers is a non-profit media organization founded in 1945 by Father James Keller, M.M. We share the message of personal responsibility and service to God and humanity with people of all faiths and no particular faith. Gifts are welcome and tax-deductible. Our legal title for wills is The Christophers, Inc.